SMILE

A User's Manual

Communicating with and about Society

Howard Giles, General Editor
University of California, Santa Barbara

"COMMUNICATING WITH AND ABOUT SOCIETY"

In the United State at least, the academic discipline of Communication has historically had a poor reputation, with many unflattering stereotypes attached to it. In years past, it was infamous for the degree an athlete might typically take if he or she was more sports-oriented than intellectually-inclined. All that has now changed, and for the better! In many colleges around the world, Communication is regarded as one of its most productive and vibrant entities. Not only do students and the lay public have more knowledge about what constitutes its subject matter, they understand it to be a rigorous study of the ways in which we convey messages in face-to-face interaction, across old and new medias, in the workplace, etc. Many Deans and Chancellors have emerged from Communication departments, a significant move that has promoted this kind of understanding and newly-found prestige. Indeed, it is a very popular discipline for even the brightest students to now take, yet one that often has the most stringent standards for a student to major in it.

All this means that to graduate with a degree in Communication allows you to obtain an array of jobs quicker than with most other degrees. Employers often love students with this background and allied sensitivities. This is due, in large part, to the fact that many of our society's ills have, rightly or wrongly, been blamed on a lack of communication, or miscommunications, between individuals and or relevant parties, be they politicians, law enforcement, or social groups relating to gender, sexual orientation, nationality, ethnicity, age, etc.

Our aim - in this quite unique international series of books - is to provide readers with an understanding of what the newly-emerging discipline of Communication has to offer society - and for each of us individually in our personal lives. The books are written by communication experts who are themselves on the cutting edge of research and theory and who are forging new advances in their respective fields. These short, reader-friendly volumes are not cluttered up by distracting academic citations and none of these appear in the text at all; classic and recent sources of further reading are provided at the end of the book. In addition, these books are not thickened by dense and complex theories, when introduced for the necessity of understanding the complexity of social issues they are introduced, again, in a digestible format.

The Series, then, is an attempt to open up a dialogue about knowledge gaps in an array of social arenas - with the conviction that furthering the public's understanding about communication issues will facilitate greater tolerance and effective, peaceful social activism. We aim to provide a feast of compelling topics from bullying to sports through to prejudice through to older life – as can be seen at the end of this Preface.

Howard Giles
University of California, Santa Barbara
General Editor

SMILE

A User's Manual

by

Piotr Szarota

Polish Academy of Sciences

Editorial Advisory Board

Dana Mastro (University of Arizona)
Peter Monge (University of Southern California)
Sik Hung Ng (City University of Hong Kong)
Lluís Pastor (Universitat Oberta de Catalunya)
Miles Patterson (University of Missouri - St. Louis)
Linda Putnam (University of California, Santa Barbara)
Maria Àngels Viladot (Universitat Oberta de Catalunya)

Copyright © 2011 by Piotr Szarota
First published in English in 2011
Design cover Marina Ysart
Cover photo: © Bigstock
© 2011 of the contents by Piotr Szarota
© 2011 of this edition by: Editorial ARESTA *www.editorialaresta.com*
ISBN: 978-84-938260-4-8
Legal Deposit: SE-1341-2011
Printed in Spain by Publidisa

All rights reserved. No part of this publication may be reproduced or distributed in any form or by any means, including, but not limited to, the process of scanning and digitization, or stored in a database or retrieval system, without the prior written permission of the Publisher.

TABLE OF CONTENTS

PROLOGUE

The smile is one of the most common facial expressions displayed by human beings. It affects our everyday interactions and can impact not only personal relationships but also business ones. Understanding the smile appears deceptively simple, yet it can be surprisingly complex.

People do smile when they're happy, but they also tend to smile when they're embarrassed, uncomfortable, and miserable or even when they're being insulted. Smiles can communicate feelings as different as love and contempt, pride and submission, easiness and awkwardness. Perhaps the most insightful comments on the smile's elusive nature can be found in Shakespeare; for instance: "One may smile, and smile, and be a villain." (Hamlet). It took some time, however, until the smile was finally considered a subject worth scientific investigation.

Over the last decade the research on smiles has really flourished. Across the world, smiling has been carefully analyzed by psychologists, primatologists, sociologists, anthropologists, and even art historians. Some scholars emphasize its importance as a primary facial expression of the positive affect, while others point to its paramount role in the process of nonverbal communication. There is still much to learn about smiling and the results of the recent research require that we take another look at long-held ideas about the smile.

Throughout the book I will point to various cultural differences in general attitude to smiling and specific smiling scenarios. It's not just to color the narrative. Smiles are so deeply embedded in culture that any attempt to understand the logic of smiling without such comparative cross-cultural frame-work would be doomed to failure. Having been brought up in Poland, where each smile has to be earned by the sweat of one's brow, it still amazes me that people in some foreign lands, like Thailand or the US may be quite indiscriminative in their smiles. I feel more at home in Spain or in France, where people seem to value their smiles more highly saving them for people they really like. But believe me; even if the similarities prevail, there are always smiles that take you by surprise.

Charles Darwin's book *The Expression of the Emotions in Man and Animals*, originally published in1872, is still a must-read for scholars interested in facial expression, but quite interestingly it was his long-forgotten grandfather, Erasmus, an English physician of the 18th century, who first commented on the origins of smile and noticed the importance of culture in the process, which could be named "smile socialization":

> In the action of sucking, the lips of the infant are closed around the nipple of his mother, till he has filled his stomach, and the pleasure occasioned by the stimulus of this grateful food succeeds. Then the sphincter of the mouth, fatigued by the continued action of sucking, is relaxed; and the antagonist muscles of the face gently acting, produce the smile of pleasure [...] Hence this smile during our lives is associated with gentle pleasure; it is visible on kittens, and puppies, when they are played with, and tickled; but more particularly marks the human features. For in children this expression of pleasure is much encouraged, by their imitation of parents, or friends; who generally address them with a smiling countenance: hence some nations are more remarkable for the gaiety and others for the gravity of their looks.

I tried to make this book informative and enjoyable at the same time. A structure is as lucid as possible. The first chapter discusses evolution of the human smile, telling the reader how it all started, roughly 2 million years ago. The next four chapters, which constitute a core of the book, examine the most important functions of the smile in the context of interpersonal communication (the smile as a signal of good will, the role of smiling in the impression management, smiling in the context of social influence and finally as expression of love and intimacy. While the previous chapters discuss the smile as an isolated social signal, in the sixth chapter the interaction between verbal and nonverbal aspects of communication will be emphasized. The smile will be finally put in the context of conversation where it usually belongs.

I will also offer a word of warning. After reading this book you might never take the smile for granted again. You might become more suspicious, more tempted to look beyond the surface of a cursory smile from your friends, colleagues, and partners. You might even try to smile more consciously and manage your smiles. The smile may never be just a smile anymore.

CHAPTER 1

Origins of the Smile

Despite the fact that academics tend to see the smile as a uniquely human phenomenon, lay people have virtually no problems in detecting smiles in animals. Not only in our closest relatives – primates – but also in dolphins, ostriches, and particularly in dogs. Even the eminent Austrian zoologist, Konrad Lorenz, a Nobel prize-winner, was absolutely convinced that his dog not only grinned happily from time to time but also laughed a lot, especially when he was in the mood to play.

We are not specifically fixated on smiles, the phenomenon is much broader. It seems that we all share uncontrollable tendency to attribute uniquely human qualities to animals and this surprising, although usually quite harmless oddity can be traced to earliest times when our bonds with nature were much stronger than today. Apparently, the anthropomorphic image of a smiling animal is particularly powerful and attractive one. But maybe there is method to our madness? Even if the smile in all its complexity is uniquely human, it's hard to overlook similarities that bond us with chimpanzees, dogs and ostriches alike.

Darwin argued that humans, like animals, have evolved patterns of signaling behavior, including facial displays. According to his theory such common signals are used to warn or invite members of the same species and on occasion other species as well.

Grin Faces and Play Faces

From the beginning of the 1950s zoologists have been looking for possible homologues of smiling, trying to detect morphologically similar face movements in our closest animal relatives. Two primate displays caught their attention immediately: the first, the *'grin'-face* or *silent bared-teeth display*; the second, the *play-face* or the *relaxed open-mouth* display. The *grin-face* is characterized by fully retracted mouth-corners and lips, and a closed or slightly opened mouth. The *play face* consists of a rather widely opened mouth and lips that remain covering the greater part of the teeth; it is often accompanied by quick and shallow breathing which may be vocalized in some species. In chimpanzees it sounds like 'ahh ahh ahh'.

Photo Bigstock

After years of research, it has been suggested that the human smile apparently evolved from the *grin-face* - primarily a ritualized submission gesture, while the *play-face*, which is associated with mock-fighting and chasing in social play, evolved into human laughter.

The grin-face or the bared-teeth display has been generally considered homologous with the human smile, not only because they look quite similar, but also based on common neurobiological wiring and similarities in the social functions of these two expressions. But it's not all that simple. It seems that communicative function of the grin-face can differ quite broadly depending on the species, their type of social organization and social context.

Among rhesus monkeys that have a despotic social system characterized by a strict hierarchy, the bared teeth display appears to be a signal of submission, or rank recognition, in that it is only given by subordinates to higher ranking individuals. Bared-teeth displays occur most often in response to the approach of a dominant monkey, and the most frequent response is for the subordinate to withdraw from any social interaction.

However, the bared-teeth display has a quite different meaning when used by species with more egalitarian social systems, including mandrills, baboons and chimpanzees. In these species, the bared-teeth display is more appeasing and functions to increase social attraction and affiliation. It communicates benign intent and no risk of aggression, but it can also occur during grooming, sexual solicitation and reconciliations, and thus helps to increase affiliative tendencies and reduce distance between individuals.

Interestingly, the social functions of grin-face vary between species in ways that are not predicted by their phylogenetic relations: Tonkean macaques use smiles almost like humans do, while chimpanzees, our much closer relatives, use it mostly for submission and appeasement. Most probably, the human smile could only evolve in a relatively egalitarian context allowing for relaxed social relationships.

A Lucky Gene and the Prehistoric Smile

For Alan Fridlund, smiling, like other facial displays, is simply a message, which influences others' behavior. According to him, vigilance for and understanding of such signals co-evolved with the signals themselves. Fridlund provided a deliberately simplistic scenario of the human smile's evolution:

> Millions of years ago, if you crossed my turf, I might bite your head off (at some risk to me, if you decided to retaliate). If you had advance warning, you might escape death trough retreat or protective defense, and we'd both survive. But you'd need cues to retreat or protect. I'd have to give them, and you'd have to notice them. Because of a lucky gene, I adventitiously bared one tooth for ½ second before I pounced. Your lucky gene made you look at my head. I bared my tooth, and you looked in the right place, not because I wanted to display my feelings, or because you wanted to see how I felt. We both acted out of pure dumb genetic luck. That we survived our skirmish increases the chances that our lucky genes will proliferate, and that my odd tooth baring and your odd vigilance for it will disseminate in our progeny.

A "lucky gene" scenario might seem a risky idea, but Fridlund points also to something which seems essential to understanding the complex nature of smiling. Smiling is generally a positive signal, often an expression of attachment or friendliness. However, it can also signal uneasiness with an uncertain social situation and a desire to overcome the problem — exactly the case with the most general use of the silent bared-teeth display by monkeys and apes.

If human smiles are analogous to the bared teeth of other higher primates, it might point to a deep-seated ambivalence in smiling. Smiles, then, are profoundly ambivalent or conflicted facial gestures, expressive of a readiness to be friendly yet associated with an atavistic display of teeth as deadly weapons. Smiling as a sign of either dominance or subordination indicates the readiness of one individual to move toward another without intending to cause physical harm even though the baring of teeth and a close approach could also precede actual fighting.

Writing about evolution of the human smile is quite tricky. We might guess how it was all possible, even write very convincing scenarios, but we will never know for sure. It has been suggested that abstract capability of language is implicated in the evolution from the silent bared-teeth display to the human smile. It's quite possible then that smiles may have played a crucial, constructive role in the evolution of speech and intelligence.

James Caron once suggested a nice framework for the analysis of laughter in historical perspective; I think it could be also very relevant if one aims to describe the evolution of the *grin face* into human smile.

In the first stage, from approximately 5 million years ago to less than 2 million years ago, hominid behavior remained very much like other higher primates. They used quite rigid and ritualized facial expressions, and among their various displays there was nothing which resembled the complexity of the human smile. The most famous fossil skeleton believed to represent an early stage of hominid evolution is widely known as Lucy. The skeleton is probably 3.2 million years old and it was classified as *Australopithecus afarensis*. Numerous portraits of Lucy tried to combine the constraints of fossil morphology with the addition of soft tissue features. However, as you might already guess, it's quite complicated to reconstruct the smile from the fossil, so we don't really know how Lucy smiled. Some scientists believed that her proto-smile resembled the bared-teeth displays of chimpanzees; others would rather point to orangutans' closed "smiles".

The second stage in the evolution of smile might have begun over 1.5 million years ago with another of our ancestors, *Homo erectus*. It seems that *Homo erectus* possessed much greater linguistic and symbol making capacity than any of his ancestors. One of the lines radiating from *Homo erectus* ended about 35 thousand years ago with the hominid commonly known as Neanderthal. Neanderthals possessed the brain size of people today, a well-developed language, and a quite elaborate culture, but they also retained primitive anatomical features, such as a face which resembles more the higher primates, than humans.

According to one theory, smiling arose as mechanisms that allowed the early hominids to adapt to the new ecological niches. Smiling might be a key factor in fostering stable and reciprocal cooperative relationships because it provided a means by which genetically unrelated individuals could reliably gauge whether another person felt positively toward them. When detecting consistent evidence of a positive affective stance in a social partner, a given hominid could more accurately predict that this particular individual was likely to respond reciprocally to cooperation. This single adaptation could foster growth of mutual positive affect between two unrelated individuals and guide them to form such bonds only with the smiling partners.

Probably at this stage the hominid smile started to change from a primitive rigid signal of motivational states to a sign functioning within a language. The Neanderthal's proto-smiling was significantly different from the silent bared-teeth display because these hominids were probably capable of such smiles which could mask, not only mirror, an individual's emotional state. Gradually our ancestors learned how to cheat. On the other hand, these newly developed social gestures probably remained relatively simple, not capable of expressing various nuanced messages in a way similar to the human smile.

The final stage in the smile evolution probably began just like stage two, with the emergence of *Homo erectus*, who not only gave rise to the Neanderthals, but was most likely the ancestor of *Homo sapiens sapiens*. The crucial factor in the development of this line was the re-organization of the neural structures which facilitated rapidly spoken language. As hominids became humans, smiling became part of the more abstract symbolic system. However, it should be emphasized that not only the quick development of neo-cortex but also the more trivial anatomical changes which took place during evolution were crucial to the development of the smile.

A development of the expressive facial muscles is a factor that could not be overstated. Some features of human expression are specific to our species thanks to the development of the muscles around the mouth and eye regions. For instance, humans, unlike higher primates, have the ability to hide their expressions with the actions of various facial muscles. Our spontaneous expressions may have an element of concealment associated with them, such as "twisting" the smile when we try to avoid appearing too pleased. This is something early hominids could only have dreamt of.

CHAPTER 2

A Message of Goodwill

Darwin speculated that a selfish character may be detectable from nonverbal cues. Today we focus more on reliable cues to altruism. There is growing evidence that smiling could act as a signal facilitating the identification of cooperative partners. The argument is that humans have an evolved capacity to read the intentions of others, along with an evolved physiological set of signaling mechanisms.

Spotting an Altruist

You'd probably agree that the idea of directly reading another's intention is quite thrilling. The problem is that reading intentions requires not only the general ability to read signals, but also some knowledge of a given person. The less we know about others, the less certain are we about their motives. But it seems that we never give up. Even when we're facing a perfect stranger, we proceed with a handful of available data, and there's always something that immediately grabs our attention.

In everyday encounters we commonly look to status, gender, and ethnicity as cues for action. In doing so, we tend to draw heavily on stereotypes about the people with whom we first meet and deal. Much could be learnt through nonverbal cues, which are displayed through clothing, gestures, and the cadence of speech. The individuals typically generate a raft of subtle signals which betray one's intention, even if that intention is being masked. In one recent study researchers used videoclips of self-reported altruists and non-altruists and found that people were doing quite well in distinguishing between the two. They never met any of the filmed individuals, so could rely only on different nonverbal signals they sent, and it appeared to be just enough to make a good decision.

Usually both inherent and intentional signals provide information and influence our strategic choices, but the most important ones typically come from the face. The eyebrow "concern furrow" is assumed to be cross-cultural signal of affiliation, but it is the smile that has been considered a crucial element in the picture.

Humans are able to recognize smiles at twice the distance of other facial expressions. Smiles can induce pleasure in the observer, but also in the smiler. More-over, people really tend to trust smiling people more than non-smiling individuals. For instance, smiling newscasters can influence political candidate choice. We also tend to trust smilers in bargaining games, and smiling defendants receive lesser sentences for a given criminal conviction.

In an industrial economy, smiling may signal trust and cooperation but it is not crucial during an economic transaction because formal institutions protect people when any dispute arises. It seems then that smiling would be much more important in small pre-industrial societies where transactions are not formally protected. In such transactions, personal trust and goodwill expressed through smiling gain prominence because they form the social glue holding the transaction together.

There is only one problem –not all smiles are equal; some appear to be much better than others. Since evolution has also provided humans with the ability to manifest a posed smile, simply trusting smiles could be quite costly since we could easily expose ourselves to possible exploitation. Only genuine smiles may be reliable indicators of likelihood to cheat. To successfully avoid cheaters we should only rely on honest signals that cannot be faked easily since the relevant neural and musculature linkages in emotional expression are physiologically constrained. It seems that this system really works, because people routinely do trust others and somehow they successfully avoid cheaters. (At least most of the time…).

Introducing the Duchenne smile

In addition to expressing positive emotion or altruistic motives, smiles serve a diverse range of communicative functions, including acting as a means to mask various emotional experiences. The smiling individual may not, therefore, always be safe to approach, especially if their expression hides malevolent intent – when intending to deceive, for example. Fortunately for the perceiver, well documented physiognomic distinctions exist between spontaneous smiles and deliberately posed smiles typically unrelated to positive emotional experience.

A crucial insight into this dual nature of smiling emerged from the rather obscure work of the French anatomist Duchenne de Boulogne. Although Duchenne's major book *Mecanisme de la physionomie humaine* (1862) was not translated into English until recently, Charles Darwin described the ideas of his French colleague in his own book on emotional expression.

Duchenne distinguished between two physically different types of smile: a supposedly natural and involuntary "genuine smile" which (apart from turning up the lips) involves tension in muscles surrounding the eyes (*orbiculares oculi*) and a fake smile, which is produced deliberately and does not activate the eyes.

In the early 1980s Paul Ekman not only adopted Duchenne's proposal but also suggested three other ways in which a genuine smile could be distinguished from other forms of smiling: 1) by the action of certain other muscles; 2) by the extent of bilateral symmetry; and 3) by the timing of the smile. They argued that genuine smiles are biologically programmed honest signals of happiness. Ekman decided to honor the French anatomist and call this expression 'the Duchenne smile'.

Despite the fact that there is no direct evidence that Duchenne smiles directly convey spontaneity (some theorists say it is rather the intensity of the stimulus that makes the smile looks more or less "genuine") there is a growing body of evidence showing that Duchenne's idea really works. Ekman found more Duchenne smiles when subjects truthfully described pleasant feelings than when they claimed to be feeling pleasant but were actually experiencing strong negative emotions. Ten-month-old infants show more Duchenne smiles when approached by their mothers than when they were approached by a stranger. Also happily married couples showed more Duchenne smiles than unhappily married couples, but there was no difference in other kinds of smiling. In another most recent study the researchers demonstrated that Duchenne smiles, by evoking positive emotions in others, are able to increase social integration and in turn reduce distress over time.

Photo Album personnel Duchenne de Boulogne
PC 4366. Fig. 1 : frontispice. Simulacre de rire naturel
Ecole Nationale Supérieure des Beaux-Arts, Paris

It seems that only enjoyment smiles specify approachability as only these expressions candidly advertise an individual experiencing positive emotion. By comparison, non-enjoyment smiles are ambiguous in that they do not uniformly relate to any specific interaction-relevant properties and therefore potentially lack utility when perceiving opportunities for interaction.

Despite all laboratory research which points to the crucial importance of the Duchenne – non-Duchenne smile differentiation, it would be premature to assume that any smiles except Duchenne ones are worthless copies, cheap fakes that could be only treated with suspicion. That's just not true. There are social smiles which have obvious pro-social components and arise from people's conscious effort to smoothen social interactions. In the next section, I show how social smiles work in three different cultural settings: the US, Japan, and Latin America.

Smiling Across Cultures

A friendly smile, so typical to US culture, is done on purpose, so it's not a "felt", Duchenne smile. Is it not genuine then? According to Duchenne de Boulogne and Ekman's standards it is not, but maybe its genuineness is based on a different premise? This smile does not reflect deep emotions, but it expresses deeply held preconceptions about social life and the nature of interpersonal relationships. It's also spontaneous because after being repeated every day it becomes an automatic response in various social contexts.

The friendly smile has its roots in American egalitarianism. Following their egalitarian beliefs, most Americans are friendly and outgoing. They feel that every single person should be treated in the same way and they are quite indiscriminate with their friendliness and smiles. Smiling is also part of American informality which is founded on the absence of formalized class system. The frequent use of the first name in addressing others (even just met strangers) is a good example. Americans tend to consider formality as somewhat pompous or even arrogant.

Americans typically socialize with many people without being close to them. They're friendly to the people they do not know well. They may spontaneously strike up a conversation with a stranger on a bus or train and they may share rather personal information with them without embarrassment. The foreigners are usually very puzzled by such an informal style of communication, which in many cultures is reserved for the close friends – as are the smiles.

There is also a strong convention to preserve surface cordiality in social interactions. Compliments and pleasant smiles are natural and expected; sharp opinions and criticism are typically avoided. This strategy aims in building a nice, friendly atmosphere. American friendliness is often misinterpreted by foreigners as a token of friendship, whereas the superficial friendliness is often used as a way to keep people at a distance. Americans like to have a nice chat with somebody they barely know, but it does not mean that they want to meet this person for a dinner. They are friendly, but at the same time they tend to avoid personal commitment, something which comes as a big surprise to many foreigners. But again it does not mean that their smiling and friendliness are not *genuine.* They might be just superficial.

To understand the social logic of smiling in Japan we should refer to another cultural concept: collectivism. In collectivistic societies people from birth onwards are integrated into cohesive groups which protect them in exchange for unquestioning loyalty. Positive emotional displays toward own groups are strongly encouraged because they facilitate group harmony. Negative emotions on the other hand, can threaten group cohesion. Small wonder, then, that the smile which is most characteristic to the collectivistic cultures of East Asia is the smile displayed when people actually feel negative i.e. socially disruptive emotions.

One of the core values of Japanese culture is *wa*, usually translated as "social harmony" or "concord". It refers to cooperation, trust, and sharing. Everybody in Japan seems to strive for *wa*. To achieve this aim one has to avoid confrontation and control her/his emotional display. The Japanese are extremely concerned with other people.

Uncontrolled display of emotion could hurt somebody's feelings and ruin social harmony, so masking one's emotions typically with a smile is common strategy. It is also true of sumo wrestlers. The story of the famous champion, Chiyonofuji could be a telling example. His consecutive winning record was suddenly stopped by another yokozuna. It is quite natural that a defeated person in that situation would be sad or regretful and almost feel like crying. However, Chiyonofuji behaved as if he were the winner and kept smiling while talking to journalists. His opponent was also interviewed. By contrast, his face remained expressionless throughout the interview. He never smiled. While it was OK for the defeated master to smile, the smile of his vanquisher would be like bragging about his victory and humiliating the rival. In a world where modesty is essential, it would be simply unacceptable.

Showing strong emotion could not only result in hurting other people but also in being ridiculed by others. The Japanese often find Americans "immature" because of the frankness with which they express their opinions and feelings. One's affect has to be controlled and subdued, and the more restrained in emotion a person is, the more he/she is respected. Interestingly this is true of not only socially disruptive emotions like anger, disgust, or contempt but also strong expressions of joy and other positive feelings, especially in "unfamiliar places".

Another way to achieve social harmony is to show submission in hierarchical relationships. Japanese employees often smile while telling superiors about their mistakes, the students smile at their teacher when they cannot answer a question. A pleasant smile is used for a manifestation of the proper degree of submission.

Such rules, however, typically don't operate for strangers. There is an interesting cross-cultural study in which behavior of Japanese and American pedestrians were analyzed. A focus was on their reactions toward a stranger who either smiled or nodded in their direction. Only 2% of Japanese smiled back, whereas 25% of Americans showed the same reaction.

Also, Chinese people do not display good feelings to all people, but only to *shuren* (lit. cooked/ripe person), namely, those they know. It would be considered strange or frivolous if someone smiles at a *shegren* (stranger). One might only guess that the smiling person is going to ask a favor or sell something.

Interestingly enough, this norm is not observed in some Asian countries such as Indonesia or Thailand, where friendliness is valued as much as in the US. It has been said that it was during the World University Games in Bangkok that the Chinese found that the "Thai smile" could be the key to staging a successful Olympics in Beijing. Actually, it was two years earlier that the Chinese capital launched a "Smile Beijing" campaign calling on its residents and future volunteers to show smiling faces to the world. "A smile is the best calling card for Beijing" was printed on blue bracelets with the Olympic Games logo, this motto coined to encourage Beijing volunteers to smile and promote the Olympic spirit.

The victory ceremony hostesses had a high standard to meet in their smiles- they had to reveal six to eight teeth when they smiled. What's more, they had to wear their smile for at least 10 minutes at a time. In the beginning, when not all of the volunteers were able to produce smiles that met the standards, they would bite down on a chopstick placed horizontally between their teeth, for an entire class period. Almost half a million people took part in this social experiment, in which they were asked to abandon their own cultural beliefs. Not only smiling to strangers, but smile showing teeth for centuries had been considered vulgar and undignified.

But if you think that collectivism is a uniquely Asian phenomenon you're very wrong. Latin American cultures are also considered collectivistic. Considerable evidence exists that many Latin American cultures emphasize harmony, social acceptance, and social support as cultural ideals. Indeed, cross-cultural psychologists have argued that these ideals are central to the concept of *simpatía* or *simpático*. *Simpático* is defined as a highly valued relational style that is based on a search for social harmony. It emphasizes expressive displays of personal charm, graciousness, and hospitality. The concept of *simpático* emphasizes the maintenance and promotion of harmonious and smooth interactions. By applying these cultural values in their everyday interactions, an individual who is simpatico behaves with respect towards others, has the ability to share others' feelings, and strives for harmony in interpersonal relations.

This latter characteristic implies a general avoidance of interpersonal conflict, and a tendency for negative behaviors to be de-emphasized in negative situations. Latin Americans resent affronts to personal dignity, such as criticism or insults. The s*impatía* script also encourages people to mask negative emotions, which might harm social harmony. Anger, irritation or contempt should be ideally well hidden under an agreeable smile. A common method of resistance to someone else's views is by means of a *pelea monga* or the relaxed fight. Rather than disagree or confront, the preferred reaction is a form of passive non-cooperation.

The qualities associated with *simpatía* are being taught from early age. When questioned about how they would react to situations that often result in aggression, Anglo-American and Mexican-American children indicated that they would confront the aggressor, whereas Mexican children indicated that they would avoid the confrontation.

This highly valued relational style resembles the search for social harmony characteristic of many East Asian cultures, but includes an emphasis on expressive displays of personal charm, graciousness, and hospitality more specific to Latin regions. The other very important cultural concept is *personalismo*, which could be roughly translated as a personalized approach. *Personalismo* refers to the degree of warmth of a personal relationship and it is grounded in the culture-based value that people are worth more than material possessions. It encourages the development of warm and friendly relationships, as opposed to impersonal or overly formal relationships. It seems that while the smile is often used purposefully as a masking strategy it also plays an important role as a sign of positive emotional attitude towards another person. Even when the interaction starts with social smiles the people are usually carried away with positive emotions.

The need for social cohesion and harmony might be even more pronounced in pre-industrial small-scale, low-income societies. In those societies, people need to cooperate with each other on a daily basis. In such contexts the display of negative emotions, such as anger or contempt, can easily disrupt social equilibrium. Here, posed or genuine smiles help to lubricate daily interactions and keep frictions from disrupting social life.

An interesting insight into the importance of smiling in the Amazonian villagers comes from the study by Ricardo Godoy. For almost a decade, he and his collaborators from Bolivia, Spain and US have been tracking native Amazonians known as the Tsimane', who live in small, remote villages tucked into the foothills of the Andes in the Bolivian Amazon. For thousands of years the Tsimane' lived like any other Amazonian society. Godoy, who lived in Lima with his Peruvian father and American mother until age fourteen, observes that in such a small-scale society that practices cross-cousin marriage people live like in one extended family and one has to quickly learn how to manage your anger and get along.

One of Godoy's recent studies explored the "mirth premium" among the Tsimane'. He and his co-workers found that people who smiled and laughed a lot had a higher body mass index (a proxy for nutritional status) and reported being healthier than their more somber counterparts. Smiling appeared to help people get along with others and to be more liked. Consequently smilers typically have better social standing and more access to resources. However it should be unfair to associate smiling with the extensive use of manipulative tactics and social machiavellism. It's more like smilers were just kinder and more generous than other people. Godoy has found that smiling is correlated with the number of gifts to others.

Researchers also tried to explain the cultural beliefs and myths associated with smiling in this Amazonian tribe:

> The Tsimane' word for smile or laughter is dyisi, which also connotes happiness or to make fun of someone. Tsimane' believe one should not smile in front of strangers because the smile might allow the stranger to bewitch the smiling person. One myth tells of a time in the past when there was no sun, and when a taboo prohibited women from smiling. Worms filled the vagina of women who broke the taboo.

Reading about specific cultural norms associated with smiling one might wonder how a tourist, a traveler or a foreign journalist should act when she or he is thrown into an unknown cultural reality and confronted with the surprised looks of not necessarily very friendly natives. The most experienced globe-trotters usually advocate using the smile as the best disarming device.

In one of his last books, *A Fortune-Teller Told Me: Earthbound Travels in the Far East*, a world famous Italian journalist, Tiziano Terzani states that it was a smile that once saved his life. As a war reporter he happened to be in Cambodia just when Khmer Rouge took control over the country. In a little border town of Poipet there were no other Westerners so he was quickly spotted by Khmer soldiers. They shouted 'CIA! CIA! America! America!' and pushed him against the wall, preparing for an execution. Terzani grabbed his passport and said with the smile: 'I'm Italian. Italian, not American!' It was all done impulsively, and he surprised even himself speaking fluent Chinese. While the local Chinese shopkeeper started translating his words he kept on smiling and waving his passport. Finally the soldiers decided to postpone an execution and wait for the political officer. When he arrived in the evening he took Terziani for interrogation. It took another couple of hours, but the Italian managed to smile even when the man aimed pistol at his head. Finally, it was over. The officer told

Terziani he was free to leave and in his impeccable French, he welcomed him in communist Cambodia.

Unfortunately, a bright smile is not always the best possible solution. There's a nice piece of advice in the Lonely Planet Guide to Poland: "Don't leave home without smile, as you won't see many on the streets. Smiling at strangers is seen here as a sign of stupidity." If you're intrigued, I will elaborate on this in the next chapter.

CHAPTER 3

Smile and Self-Presentation

The impression management is the process through which people try to control the impressions other people form of them. It is often used synonymously with self-presentation. In his seminal book *The Presentation of Self in Everyday Life* Erving Goffman presents impression management dramaturgically using the imagery of the theatrical performance. According to him there are two main motives that govern self-presentation: instrumental and expressive. Instrumental, because we want to influence others and gain rewards. Expressive, since we construct an image of ourselves to claim a specific personal identity and then we present ourselves in a manner that is consistent with that image.

A classic typology describes five types of self-presentation strategies. A person who'd like to appear likeable will probably chose an **ingratiation strategy** which includes doing favors, being agreeable, and paying compliments. A person who seeks to appear competent will choose a **self-promotion strategy,** emphasizing own strengths and achievements. A person who wants to appear worthy will use an **exemplification strategy,** claiming high moral values. A person who would like to be perceived as helpless will probably resort to a **supplication strategy**; this might include appearing weak to evoke nurturance or claiming incompetence to avoid responsibility. Finally, a person who seeks to look powerful and dangerous will use an **intimidating strategy** and demonstrate power and ability to inflict harm.

Usually facial expression and other nonverbal signals are no less important in achieving these goals than verbal statements. Body posture, hand gestures, and facial displays may help in presenting oneself in the appropriate way. However achieving the consistent image sometimes might be tricky. One clumsy move, one unconvincing line and we might get booed off the stage.

Choosing the right costume and right mask is absolutely essential. Most of them fit only certain roles; there are only a few that are quite universal. Take spectacles – if you choose massive horn-rimmed frames, they might help you become the intellectual neurotic, Woody Allen style; with colorful granny glasses you may pass for the bohemian, arty person; and if you find some nice and fancy Ray Bans you may even look cool and sexy. The fact that the smile might easily fit all five strategies of self-presentation may come as a big surprise; the smile after all is primarily a signal of good will. However, as I pointed out in the previous chapters, the nature of smiling is far from being that simple.

When a person uses an ingratiation strategy, the smile which would ideally fit the picture is the agreeable smile of a flatterer. This smile should not be too assertive, but also not too shy. A friendly display that is easily recognizable, but not too imposing. Nice, but easily forgettable.

Exemplification would instead require a benevolent smile of compassion and forgiveness, the smile that the Dalai Lama so perfectly and effortlessly mastered. It is not the smile for beginners; it is so easy to blow it. Some politicians exercise it on election billboards but those smiles usually just don't feel quite right. Most of the time, it's like bad acting. Maybe you just have to be born like that?

Photo Bigstock

In self-promotion strategy, the best choice would be the bold smile of self-assurance. It is a smile of a winner. Broad grin might be a good choice, but you have to be careful or you risk overkill. Sometimes there is only a thin line between appearing assertive and appearing pompous. There must be much substance behind this smile.

Supplication would require something completely different, and one should resort to a shy or even miserable smile. Again there's a big risk of overkill. If you try too hard you might not only avoid responsibility in the particular situation – the intended effect – but also prove to be incompetent and hopeless.

And what about intimidation? Initially the smile here may seem totally out of place, and actually people often use a stern non-smiling face as a default facial expression corresponding with intimidation tactics. But a devilish grin of menace may prove even more effective as an intimidation device. It is the scary smile to which the most evil of film villains sometimes resort. What comes to mind is Jack Nickolson's smile in *The Shining* or the menacing grin of Heath Ledger's Joker in *The Dark Knight.*

At first, these five types of smiling might look quite similar, and the messages they carry would typically be fully recognizable only in context. To be really convincing they should be synchronized with other non-verbal signs. You go for self-promotion, your head has to be tilted up, posture quite relaxed, and eyes should never wonder about or look down. If you're more into intimidation you have to go a little bit further. Staring eyes with a hint of madness would make a nice addition. What's also important is clothing. I mentioned the specs, but clothing itself is even more essential. It's all about theatre, after all. Even seemingly trivial details could be decisive in the process of making a fully believable character. You might remember the Coen Brothers' film *No Country for Old Men* and the brilliant performance by Javier Bardem. It's a crazy haircut that makes the actor's transformation into a psychopath hitman persona so terrific and convincing.

Of course, no less important is the "content". The words we speak, the thoughts we express, the ideas we create. Even the most perfect non-verbal self-presentation will not work without the appropriate line. Smiles like other gestures usually work as a part of the communication process, and they should be nicely synchronized with words. This problem will be examined in detail in the Chapter Six.

It is very unlikely to stick to the same expression no matter what the context is. The Joker did it but is it really an example we would be thrilled to follow? Self-presentation strategies usually differ from situation to situation, so the same person may smile differently when interacting with a father-in law, a spouse, and own children. Actually it's even more complicated. In the next section I discuss how smiling could be utilized in the context of job interview, political campaign, and Internet dating.

Smiling To Get a Job

In this paragraph I will discuss importance of the candidate's smile in a personnel selection procedure. Nonverbal communication plays an important part in the hiring interview from both the applicant's and the interviewer's perspectives.

Many applicants consider carefully what they are going to say during the interview, but only few take into account the nonverbal cues they should manage to control. Too bad, since this may seriously affect their chances. Research on the role of nonverbal cues in the hiring interview suggests that applicants displaying more expressive visual nonverbal behaviors, and cues of nonverbal immediacy, such as frequent eye contact and smiling receive more favorable evaluations than non-expressive interviewees. The savvy applicant engages in careful impression management, constantly monitoring verbal responses to emphasize job-related strengths and hide what might be perceived as a weakness.

Interestingly, the interviewer's nonverbal behavior can also play an important part in influencing the applicant's behavior. In an interesting study, interviewers behaved in either a *cold* or *warm* manner (with much more eye contact and more smiling). It appeared that applicants interviewed by the nonverbally warm interviewer were judged as performing better than applicants in the cold interview condition.

Employers imposing the smile requirement may also use it as an employee selection tool. In US the ability to smile nicely to the customers is typically considered essential in a service sector. As one American manager noted, "I tell my retail managers that if they don't smile, don't hire them. I don't care how well educated they are, how well they are versed in retail, if they can't smile, they're not going to make a customer feel welcome. And we don't want them in our store".

It's difficult to overestimate the role of gender stereotypes and gender-role expectations in smiling. Gender-role expectations are socially shared ideas concerning the behavior and characteristics regarded as desirable for men and women. Such expectations also influence the perception of the occupations that are usually performed either by men or by women. For the proper performance of occupations that are usually held by women ('feminine' occupations, such as pediatric nurse), stereotypical feminine characteristics are seen as necessary, and for the proper performance of occupations usually held by males ('masculine' occupations, such as policeman), stereotypical masculine characteristics are seen as necessary. Thus, masculine occupations are considered to be more appropriate for men, and feminine occupations more appropriate for women.

In accordance with gender-role expectations, women are strongly oriented towards and interested in others, whereas men are expected to be autonomous, assertive, task-oriented, and emotionally reserved. A focus on social relations is considered to be more suitable for women than for men, consequently all occupations in which social contact is important are considered to be more appropriate for women than men.

Because gender-role expectations are socially shared expectations, they usually guide not only a selection board's evaluation criteria but also candidates' strategic decisions concerning how should they look and behave. In the interesting Dutch study each participant was presented with an advertisement for a job and was asked to imagine that he or she wanted that particular job. In addition, each participant was photographed and asked to imagine that this photo would be sent with their job application. They were requested to ensure that the impression they wanted to make in order to get the job would be captured by the photo. In such a context, participants can strategically go along with the expectations of the selector. It was expected that the participants would smile more in response to a feminine than to a masculine job, and that women would smile relatively more in response to a feminine job, whereas men would smile relatively less in response to a masculine job. The results do not support these expectations, however women smiled more when social contact was emphasized in a job description. Additionally men and women smiled more in response to a low-status job than to a high-status job. The characteristics which were regarded as relevant to the impression the participants wanted to make in relation to the high-status jobs indicate that they wanted to come across as independent and professional. The characteristics that were important for the low-status jobs suggest that, in relation to these jobs, the participants wanted to give the impression that they were agreeable.

The result that women smile more in response to a feminine low-status job for which social contact is important indicates that women react in a more pliable, differentiated manner than men do. Women adjust their smiles to the different aspects of the job which are consistent with gender-role expectations whereas the smiling behavior displayed by men seems not to be guided by such norms. These results suggests that women have a more subtle idea of the expectations of their interaction partners, and further that they are better able than men to monitor their smiling behavior according to these expectations.

Even more interesting are the results of research focused on job interview dynamics. In a recent American study mock job interviews were conducted and videotaped. It was found that the female participants tended to fake smiles to mask negative emotion and to appear enthusiastic, more than the male participants did. Asked why they were faking smiles, they reported that they wanted to please the interviewer. Men, however, tended to be less other-focused when smiling, reporting that they "wanted to appear like a nice person," or that they were amused at something that was said. The power of gender-role expectations was also evident here.

A nice, humble smile may help in finding a low-status job, but smiling may also be detrimental, even for women who are generally expected to smile more than men. In one study, male interviewers sexually harassed real female job applicants, asking about such things as their attitude toward going bra-less in the workplace. In the abstract, most women say they would express outrage at such a question, but with a job at stake, not a single applicant objected. Instead, they often smiled and answered the inappropriate questions - apparently they decided to appear pleasant and competent even while having to contend with sexual harassment. The amount of non-Duchenne smiling was positively correlated with the degree to which participants reported feeling angry, upset, disgusted, and irritable and was negatively correlated with feeling strong. In addition, non-Duchenne smiling was positively correlated with perceiving the interviewer as sexist and perceiving the interview as having been sexually harassing. Their smiles indicated not amusement but an attempt to get through an untenable situation. Going along may have seemed like the best way to get ahead, but apparently it was clearly not the case. People looking at videotapes of those interviews (with the sound switched off) rated the polite smilers as less competent and less intelligent. The more a woman smiled, the less favorable the ratings were.

Maybe those fake smiles were simply misinterpreted? Research shows that such misinterpretation was certainly the case – but only by male participants. Interestingly, men were significantly less accurate in the interpretation of different smile types displayed by the interviewed women and the errors were in seeing any smile as indicating genuine feeling. Thus they probably thought that the harassed women were clearly enjoying themselves. It's no wonder that they rated them as they did, but this male tendency to misinterpret women's smiles is very alarming.

Smiling To Win Friends

Personal warmth, approachability, friendliness, and agreeableness: these qualities seem even more important in a situation in which we plan to impress a potential friend or date. Anyone who writes on the smile in the context of interpersonal communication cannot ignore Dale Carnegie's book *How to Win Friends and Influence People.* The entirety of Chapter 2, entitled: *A Simple Way to Make a Good First Impression,* is dedicated to the smile. It opens quite dramatically:

> At a dinner party in New York, one of the guests, a woman who had inherited money, was eager to make a pleasing impression on everyone. She had squandered a modest fortune on sables, diamonds and pearls. But she hadn't done anything whatever about her face. It radiated sourness and selfishness. She didn't realize what everyone knows: namely, that the expression one wears on one's face is far more important than the clothes one wears on one's back.

It's easy to dismiss the book as shallow and manipulative, however Carnegie's advice proved quite effective. Numerous studies have found that smiling individuals tend to be rated as more likeable, friendly, and sociable, as well as more competent and intelligent. Smiling individuals are perceived not only as happier, but also as more carefree, and more relaxed. Further, the frequency of smiling by an individual affects the amount of warmth perceived by others. In addition, smiling increases ratings of attractiveness. The positive effect of smiling was found not only in the US, but also in Hong Kong, Japan, Brazil, and Poland.

cross-cultural

But despite Carnegie's advice, and the empirical evidence, many people seem to underestimate the power of smiling. In a recent study, I analyzed cross-cultural differences in preference for social smiling among the users of one of the most popular instant messaging sites called Windows Live Messenger (formerly known as MSN Messenger, and often referred to as MSN), which is now available in more than 60 countries and in 26 languages. Windows Live Messenger allows you to find new acquaintances or on-line dates. First, you have to introduce yourself; your photo will be put alongside personal information such as age, family status, hobbies, etc.

Of course, we will never be sure how sincere MSN users are in presenting themselves, but it could be assumed that they are quite strongly motivated to present themselves in a way that would gain them someone's attention or sympathy. Many Internet dating sites openly encourage the users to smile in order to increase their attractiveness. The British dating service (see: http://www.date.co.uk) advises: "The best photos for posting are those that feature nice *head shots.* These photos (usually taken from the shoulders up) are used most successfully in your profile as the first photo people see [...].And if you're taking new photos just for us, **remember to give a great big smile for the camera**".

Overall 3,000 photographs from 20 countries were analyzed. There were places where a vast majority (over 75%) presented a smiling face; it was the case in Brazil, USA, and Indonesia. But there were places where the smile apparently does not seem appropriate in this context. In Poland less than 40 % of the photos included a smiling face.

I realized that the answer lies in specific cultural norms which guide the decisions of the MSN users in different countries. What makes Poles so resistant to smile is probably their preoccupation with sincerity, at least when it comes to expressing their own feelings. To be sincere is to present one's feelings truthfully, to say and show what one really feels. As a Polish linguist, Anna Wierzbicka puts it:

> In Poland the assumption that a person's face should reflect his or her feelings is far more than an individual preference: it is a cultural premise, supported by linguistic evidence in the form of pejorative expressions like *fałszywy uśmiech* (a false smile) and *sztuczny uśmiech* (artificial smile) [...]. Such expressions imply that someone is *displaying good feelings towards another person* that in fact are not felt, and that *of course* it is very bad to do so.

A Polish smile usually indicates not general friendliness but real affection and is used only with those persons one knows and really likes. It is possible then that Poles (or at least many of them) simply refuse to be involved in any kind of self-promotion games, because what they really want is to appear natural. Moreover they probably strive to appear natural every time they are being photographed so actually they might not have a spare smiling photo which could be put on-line.

The fact that in many countries people use the English word "cheese" to simulate a smile in front of the camera does not mean that the ethic and aesthetic of the toothy smile are valid for all cultures. Poles for instance have no equivalent to "Say cheese" and they are still bit hesitant to smile to the camera. Also in Arab culture, saying cheese to the camera is not a common practice. As the Lebanese anthropologist, Fuad Khuri comments:

> When an American poses for a photograph, he says 'cheese' to create a false smile. An Arab, by contrast, puts on a serious look as if he were facing the Day of Judgment. A photograph in Arabia is a public image, and in public no 'cheese' is permissible.

But, quite interestingly, the differences in the preference for smiling in instant-messaging conversations might have been also analyzed in a geopolitical context. A significant difference in the number of smiles in Western and Eastern European samples was found, with the former Eastern Europeans (Poles, Czechs, Slovenians, Hungarians, and Germans from the former GDR) smiling less than Western Europeans (British, French, Italians, Spaniards, Finns, and Germans from the former West Germany). These differences may be directly influenced by the users' well-being or they may be due to different behavioral strategies.

There some empirical support in favor of the first explanation. In a study conducted just before the fall of the Berlin wall, scientists observed workers who enjoyed themselves in bars on both sides of the city. They focused on the behavioral signs consistent with depression and found that West Berliners smiled significantly more often than East Berliners, they also look more relaxed. It seems that workers from the former GDR might have been more depressed than their counterparts from the West.

The second explanation might evoke a concept of post-communist mentality; i.e. East Europeans as less assertive, less friendly and more distrustful, and therefore less eager to smile than Western Europeans. In her book *Café Europa. Life After Communism*, the Croatian writer Slavenka Drakulic (1997) describes the "non-smiling culture" of Eastern Europe and links it directly to the post-communist mentality:

> Here a smile is a sign not of courtesy, but of the inferiority of the smiler … Not so long ago, a smile could provoke distrust. Why is that person smiling? Does it mean that he or she is happy – how is that possible, with all this misery around us? A show of happiness was a reason to suspect a person – at best it was considered indecent.

Smiling To Win Elections

At first, the situation of a politician preparing an election campaign seems very similar to the one of the Internet user aiming to win new friends online. Politics however is a little more complicated than surfing. First, a political campaign involves a large group of people, and a politician is rarely left to her/his own devices. Secondly, the politician's image is not presented solely by photographs, and is not only to be found on the Internet, but also on TV, and outdoor billboards. An objective is to reach as many people as possible; everyone is considered as a potential voter.

Even a single photograph can have a clear impact on voters' judgments regarding a candidate's competence, attractiveness, likeability, and integrity. People process visual symbols more quickly and efficiently than written texts. Visual symbols potentially contain more information than other symbol types, yet viewers remember visuals more easily than the verbal narration. Like it or not, people believe what they see more than what they hear or read.

Photographs and other visual materials enable voters to form impressions, opinions, and beliefs about political candidates. According to impression management theory, positive impressions will eventually lead to equally positive outcomes. In effect, politicians recognize that specific images are needed to convince the voter. The desired outcome in impression management is the projection of an image of competency, motivation, and productivity.

Nonverbal visual cues that can promote likeability and attractiveness are positive affect cues, such as smiles, head nods, and raising eyebrows. The more a person smiles and nods his or her head, the better they are liked and the more attractive they will appear. It does not mean, however, that the one who smiles the most wins an election.

There are at least two important tips which might prove decisive in a political struggle. First, one should know how to smile. This is true of Internet daters as well, but for politicians knowing how to smile can make or break a career. Since the late 1970s experts in political marketing have fully acknowledged the importance of the genuine smile. An unfelt and seemingly forced smile will not do the trick. Although Jimmy Carter's toothy smile once became emblematic and his campaign buttons showed just teeth with the caption 'The Grin Will Win', he ultimately lost his run for the second term. His Southern grin, although very impressive seemed bit strained and much less sincere than an effortless smile of a professional actor, Ronald Reagan. Especially in the aftermath of the spectacular fiasco of the 1980 Tehran military operation, orchestrated by Carter's administration.

Photo Library of Congress

The election smile should ideally be warm and relaxed yet at the same time dominant. It's not easy to achieve, however. Dominance has generally been associated with no or less smiling, but specific eyebrow positioning together with other nonverbal cues such as head position (i.e. straight, head tilting is considered an appeasement gesture) might make the smiling face more dominant than non-smiling expression. There is little disagreement, however, over how the dominant smile should look. In Canada, it was the weak smile that was found to be the model expression for communicating dominance; in Brazil, it was the broad smile. Apparently there are some cultural differences in the way we perceive different types of smiling.

Another point that should be made here is the importance of context. The smile should always be appropriate, i.e. suitable for a particular occasion. The political candidate who smiles a lot but doesn't know when to stop will probably blow his chances. Interestingly in 2000 US presidential campaign Al Gore and George W. Bush both presented photographs without a smile. This technique was employed deliberately to illustrate concern for the needs of the people.

However, it should be noted that even the most appropriate smile might be easily manipulated and put into the wrong context. This is a quite simple and relatively effective way to discredit a political opponent. Probably the first attempt comes from the US 1968 presidential campaign. There was a television ad which presented a smiling Democratic Candidate, Hubert Humphrey, juxtaposed with images of the Vietnam War and domestic rioting during the Democratic National Convention. Voters could have interpreted this as a lack of concern by Humphrey for significant national problems. Eventually it was not smiling Humphrey, but frowning Nixon who won the election.

While it is hard to imagine a stern politician from the modern American perspective, the grinning leaders are a relatively recent invention. John F. Kennedy and Jimmy Carter were famous for their smiles, but it was Reagan who first smiled for an official portrait in 1981. All the later presidents follow suit.

In Europe, there has long been resistance towards the American smiling agenda in politics. An eminent French philosopher, Jean Baudrillard, was quite bemused watching Reagan's election campaign. For him, hugely critical towards US social reality and politics, Reagan's smile is quintessentially an American smile:

> This smile signifies only the need to smile. It is a bit like the Cheshire Cat's grin: it continues to float on faces long after all emotion has disappeared [...] The smile of immunity, the smile of advertising: 'This country is good. I am good. We are the best'. It is also Reagan's smile – the culmination of self-satisfaction of the entire American nation – which is on the way to becoming the sole principle of the government. Smile to show how transparent, how candid you are. Smile if you have nothing to say.

This European perspective changed considerably during the last decade. In 1994, Silvio Berlusconi easily imitated the American grin, followed by Tony Blair and, most recently, Nicolas Sarkozy. However, there are still seats of resistance. When I compared photos from the European Parliament election campaign of June 2009, significant differences in the amount of smiles on the election photos from Britain, France, Spain, Germany and Poland emerged. While most of the British, French, Spanish and German candidates decided to smile at the voting public, only half of the Polish candidates did the same. In Poland, politicians are still expected to look serious and the smile is quite often seen as a sign of weakness or immaturity.

There is also not much smiling among political leaders from Southern and Eastern Asia. The concept of the assertive smile is quite alien to this region's cultures. In most of these Asian countries, the smile is rather associated with appeasement than with dominance. Smiling is typically a vehicle for showing respect and compliance to the superior; the faces of the mandarins, kings, and Party leaders usually remain expressionless.

While Thais are known for their seductive smiles (I will elaborate on this in Chapter Six), their king, Bhumibol has been seldom seen smiling. From the biographical account, "The King Never Smiles" we can learn that in Buddhist culture, either a smile or a frown would indicate attachment to worldly pleasures or desires, something which is generally not expected from the person so much admired and venerated. It is small wonder then that King Bhumibol's public image has always been one of kindly benevolence and impassivity. Just like the images of the greatest kings of the past.

CHAPTER 4

The Smile That Sells

The notion of having a friendly staff and providing "service with a smile" has gradually become a mantra for service sector at least in the English speaking countries. In the US, this started as early as 19th century, when commercial advice literature began to flourish. The manuals pointed to the importance of appearance and self-discipline, but it was a "sunny personality" which was assumed a crucial element in a big struggle for success. Salesmen themselves soon found out that the smile could really work miracles and some of them could not help writing ecstatic yet somewhat clumsy poems celebrating this discovery:

> I smile because I know it pays.
> It means dollars and cents in many ways.
> To me, life has not been 'One long song'
> There's many a thing that has gone wrong.
> But I don't peddle troubles where're I go.
> For who wants to hear my tale of woe?
> I can't sell goods with a hard luck tale,
> So I smile, keep happy, and make my sale.

One of the most recent, most radical, and probably most ridiculous inventions in the field is the Smile Scan. The device scans a person's face, renders a 3D model of it and checks a few critical spots, most importantly mouth and eyes regions to evaluate if someone is smiling well enough. Every smile gets a score from 0% to 100%. Those with a below-par grin, are kindly advised by the system: "Lift up your mouth corners". If they don't try hard enough they get a reprimand: 'You still look too serious!'

It may look like a bad joke, but journalists reported that a growing number of Japanese service industries are reportedly using the new Smile Scan system for "smile training" among its staff. In some companies workers receive a print out of their daily smile which they will be expected to keep with them throughout the day to inspire them to smile at all times. For those who search for perfection a popular game for the hand-held Nintendo DS called "Face Training" provides a full exercise regime.

In this chapter I will focus on the contemporary uses and misuses of the smile for commercial purposes. I will discuss the phenomenon of emotional contagion and different techniques of emotional labor. Essentially, I will show how printed and television advertising capitalize on the power of smile.

Smiling is Contagious!

"Emotional contagion" is defined as the flow of emotions from one person to another, with the receiver "catching" the emotions that the sender displays. Of course, you can be lucky and catch joy or excitement, but if you're not lucky enough you might end up catching something definitely less tempting, such as irritation or sadness –usually not the best catch of the day. In the context of service interactions, emotional contagion creates a ripple effect of emotions from service employees to customers, and there are typically positive emotions flying here.

Despite the fact that most people experience emotional contagion every day, for some of us it may seem like something closer to magic than psychology. The research shows the process of emotional contagion can be attributed to people's tendency to automatically mimic and synchronize facial expressions with those of another person. This type of emotional contagion is driven by a two-step mimicry process, in which a person spontaneously imitates another person's expressions, which leads the person to experience the same emotions.

Emotional contagion theories suggest that "primitive emotional contagion" is spurred by the extent to which the sender displays emotions; a greater emotional display by the sender results in higher levels of emotional contagion in the receiver. In contrast, "conscious emotional contagion" is based on social comparison processes in which people actively search for emotions as a type of social information. This activity grows particularly strong in ambiguous situations, when people are not quite sure how they are supposed to act. Unlike primitive emotional contagion, conscious emotional contagion is determined less by the frequency of smiling and more by genuineness of the smiles. When the receiver perceives the sender's emotional display as merely fake, he or she will not interpret the emotional display as adequate for reducing perceived ambiguity. In this case emotional contagion is less likely to occur.

In the context of customer service it is the primitive emotional contagion which may most likely occur, and the extent of a service employee's positive emotional display (e.g. amount of smiling) seems to be a crucial factor. If an employee increases his or her amount of smiling, customers are more likely to mimic these facial expressions unconsciously during the encounter and ultimately altering their own emotional state. However, the authenticity of the service employee's display of positive emotions may influence the customer's emotional state.

And here we're have to come back to the famous Duchenne smile, which was introduced in Chapter Two. Felt smiles do stimulate more positive emotional reactions by respondents than "faked" smiles. The status of genuine smiling has been also confirmed in marketing research. The authenticity of smiling, rather than its extent, influences the customer's emotions and perceptions. High authenticity results in a significantly greater increase in the change in customer positive affect. Moreover, a customer's satisfaction tends to be higher when customers perceive employee's behavior as authentic.

Interestingly, the smiles in the service sector are usually considered important not only in face to face interaction with the customer but also when the contact is mediated by telephone. The fact that smiling may have been quite easily inferred based solely on vocal cues is generally acknowledged by lay people, but until recently there has been little research supporting this insight. Smiles have been well researched as visual displays, but much less investigation has been conducted into their vocal expression.

What we know is that smiles and other expressions of happiness are linked to a general rise in pitch. However, it has also been demonstrated that pitch is not necessary for smile discrimination as listeners can still identify smiles in whispered speech. The acoustical cues that listeners utilize may be derived from prototypical ideals about what smiles are expected or believed to sound like. Strange, isn't it? What's even more interesting, people can hear smiles even when monosyllabic nonsense-words are spoken. They do not need any story to help them in the process of 'smile deduction'.

The recent British study investigated this problem in more detail. It appeared that listeners can, with varying degrees of success, hear various types of smiles in the voices of strangers in the absence of visual cues. Participants who listened to the carefully prepared audio clips appeared to be very good at discriminating between fragments recorded with and without smiling, but the main revelation is the fact that they could also discriminate between Duchenne and social smiles. Apparently social smiles which serve an appeasement or politeness function may have offered fewer vocal cues to aid listeners in the characterization of the smile. It seems that from now on the employees will be trained not only to smile by the phone, but to send genuine smiles.

Most recently new revelations regarding the contagious nature of smiling have been published. Researchers found that happiness spreads across a diverse array of social ties, from spouses to siblings to neighbors. They found that nearby ties had a far greater influence than distant ties: for example, knowing someone who is happy, makes you 15.3% more likely to be happy, but having happy next-door neighbors makes you a full 34% more likely to be happy. While the researchers think that face-to-face connection is important in spreading happiness (hence the decline of these effects with distance), they did a separate study of Facebook profiles, where they found that people smiling in their photographs had more Facebook friends and that more of those friends were themselves smiling. Although the researchers admitted that smiling is different than happiness, it was as close as they could come in the virtual world.

Smile Labor

"Emotional labor" refers to service employees' display of expected emotions; it should be noted however, that it is not always a *positive* emotion which is expected to be displayed. The display of positive emotions is required in many service occupations, including restaurant workers and flight attendants. Funeral directors, in contrast, are usually expected to be less cheerful; they may smile but preferably not at work! The emotional labor could be even more complicated if switching from positive to negative emotions is expected according to different scenarios. Debt collectors, for instance, are taught to express warmth with anxious debtors, calmness with aggressive ones, and irritation with reluctant customers.

With regard to specific emotional labor strategies, scholars have drawn on distinction between surface acting and deep acting as the primary framework for service employees. In 'surface acting,' an employee tries to change only the outward behavior to exhibit the required emotions. Thus, surface acting refers to the act of displaying an emotion that is not felt and could involve both suppression of felt emotions and faking of unfelt emotions. For example, when dealing with an annoying customer, a waitress may simply put on a smile and pretend to be friendly without actually feeling anything positive. To put it simple, surface acting lacks authenticity.

Photo Bigstock

With 'deep acting,' however, employees express expected (or required) emotions by attempting to create these emotions within themselves. This strategy is similar to the method-acting technique developed by famous Russian director Constantin Stanislavski in which actors are taught to create self-induced true emotions by using their emotional memory and recalling prior experiences and emotions. Stanislavski's ideas inspired some of the greatest film actors of the last century like Marlon Brando, Robert De Niro and Dustin Hoffman, but prove very effective also in the mundane context of service delivery. American flight attendants are often trained to deal with angry passengers by thinking of them as frightened, first time fliers. This process enables the flight attendants to change their inner feelings toward the customer from annoyance to pity and sympathy.

Deep acting is generally considered a better option when it comes to smiling. The value of the genuine smile is once again acknowledged. Strained or forced smiles are not only considered inferior but also critical to the company's reputation because they might too easily detected by customers. As one of the American airline companies put it in its ad, "Our smiles are not just painted on. Our flight attendants' smiles will be more human than the phony smiles you're resigned to seeing on people who are paid to smile".

Smiling seems to be an easy and enjoyable job, but the emotional labor, even if it is just smiling, is considered not only difficult but might deteriorate your health. Scientist already acknowledged the problem. Quite recently one of the leading Japanese psychiatrists decided to educate general public about the psychological costs involved in smiling:

> "Forcing yourself to wear this smile mask for a long period of time can, as it gets more extreme, lead to real depression. The all-day smiles are also responsible for a range of physical ailments: among the patients that he has treated with smile-mask syndrome, many complain of painful muscle and head-aches akin to repetitive strain injury. Depression, mental illness and other disorders are spreading fast and smile-mask syndrome could soon become a serious national health issue."

The employees who engage in surface acting are usually more emotionally exhausted than those who were trained for deep acting. Generally, the more autonomy a service worker has, the less harmful the effects of emotional labor. The burden of the forced smile became the subject of a lawsuit filed by employees against their employer, Safeway, one the largest supermarket chains in the United States. In the early 1990s, Safeway had implemented the smile as a way to improve customer service. The fallout came as employees complained that male customers often misinterpreted the smiles for sexual invitation and harassed them. Employees opted for the choice, which they were obviously denied; as one of them put it "Let me decide who I am going to say hello to with a big smile."

In his bestselling book, *How to Win Friends and Influence People*, which I already mentioned in the previous chapter, Dale

Carnegie asserted that a smile as a messenger of goodwill is indispensable in service encounters. In his own words, we should smile even when we don't feel like it, because action and feeling go together. To emphasize the universal value of his insights, Carnegie quoted a Chinese proverb: "A man without a smiling face must not open a shop". It may come as a big surprise for anyone who happened to visit mainland China or its more Westernized provinces. As James Watson notes:

> In Hong Hong people are suspicious of anyone who displays what is perceived to be an excess of congeniality. 'If you buy an apple from a hawker and he smiles at you' – my Cantonese tutor once told me, 'you know you're being cheated'.

One of the most interesting cases of a service-related cultural misunderstanding was the conflict between Korean shop owners and Black customers in the Crenshaw neighborhood of Los Angeles, which in the early 1990s resulted in numerous incidents of racial hatred and fierce riots. In the interviews conducted soon after these events African-Americans described how they felt disrespected in immigrant Korean stores, pointing to the lack of smiles and small talk routines. The problem is that the types of behavior which many African-Americans might interpret as signs of sociable involvement in service encounters are actually considered an imposition and a sign of poor manners by Koreans.

In Japan it was not until the 1980s that people smiled in the workplace at all. The first "perma-smiles" have been introduced to the Japanese in 1983 by the employees of the newly founded Disneyland. In 1990s in Japan as well as in South Korea the first smile schools have been established. The aim of the smile trainings has been to teach how to make the smile look genuine. Formal smiles were never a problem, especially in Japan, but there were missing important ingredient: authenticity. They were also closed and weak and the new service standards asked for the open, toothy smile, completely alien to East Asian tradition. "Not only do customers buy more when they get a warm and fuzzy feeling from clerks, but employee morale rises and absenteeism declines, asserts Japanese "smile guru", author of the book "Power of a Laughing Face" and president of his own company, the Smile Amenity Institute.

The idea of service with a smile was also implemented in Europe, but not everywhere very successfully. In 1965, France launched the "National Campaign for Reception and Friendliness" to improve the image of the country in the eyes of Americans, who typically perceived French people as rude and hostile. Booklets of "smile checks" (*cheques-sourire*) were distributed among tourists. When they felt they received particularly good service at a hotel, restaurant, or elsewhere, they were to tear out one of their ten smile checks, inscribe the name and institution of the friendly employee, and then mail it to the government's tourist office. At the end of the season, the government would award the ten most-honored French workers with vacation trips of their own. The experiment can't have been particularly successful, because quite recently the French tried it again. In July 2009, the tourist board established a new campaign: "Paris smiles for you!" to welcome visitors. To that end, there are now stands staffed by teams of "smile ambassadors" at popular city spots . Who knows, maybe it will work this time.

In Europe, the French are not alone in their approach to smiling. In a book *Spain is Different*, targeted at American visitors we find a whole paragraph on smiling:

> Spaniards who go to the United States are struck by friendliness of Americans. One Catalan who moved to the U.S. complained that his face hurt from having to smile so much [...] In Spain, in contrast, public decorum implies seriousness. Except at fiesta time, people tend to go without smiles on their faces. Don Quixote was known as the Knight of the Sad Countenance, and in the days of the greatness of Spain's colonial empire, King Philip II set the style of sober black clothes with a plain white ruff around the neck and the unsmiling face. Spaniards at that time were known all over Europe for their serious demeanor.

Spanish psychologists would probably agree with this description. Some time ago couple of them went to the famous Prado Gallery in Madrid to analyze what facial expressions are to be found on the classical, predominantly Spanish paintings. They concluded that in the old days the smile was not considered a symbol of joy or happiness but rather uncouthness. The only smiles that were found were the smiles of boors, drunkards and lunatics.

But those were painted smiles by Velazquez and Goya. What about 'service with a smile' in a contemporary Spain? In the same book the author tells the story of an American going to a tobacco shop to buy some stamps. He is being served by an attractive young shop assistant. Impressed by her appearance, he tries out all his charms, but her manners remain cool and distant. However, she greets other customers with a smile. He expected the American treatment, but in Spain it simply doesn't work. No smile for strangers. But there's nothing to worry about, since in Spain a stranger is no longer a stranger after the first encounter. From this decisive moment the relationship is *Ya nos conocemos* (We know each other), and smiles are quite possible, however not obligatory.

Advertising with a Smile

It has long been known that associating a product with positive emotions, by, for example, presenting it alongside a pleasantly smiling beautiful model, soon leads to the object itself being associated with those positive feelings. Indeed, the more positive a perceiver's emotional reaction to an advertised product, the more positively he or she evaluates that product.

Typically research on smiles in marketing and advertising focuses only on the presence or absence of a smile and the results of these studies are usually interpreted in terms of emotional contagion. Fair enough. The problem is it only works from time to time. We may only guess that the disparity of findings can be attributed to the fact that some of these studies involve genuine smiles of enjoyment and some involve non-enjoyment smiles.

This problem was directly addressed in a recent American study in which participants were asked how they like T-shirts presented by models with different facial expressions. T-shirts were evaluated more positively when they were paired with a genuine smile than when paired with a fake smile or neutral expression. The more positive product evaluations were only seen for those T-shirts paired with genuine smiles; items paired with posed smiles were evaluated in a manner identical to those paired with a neutral facial expression. Apparently a posed smile was essentially responded to by participants as if it were emotionless. Importantly, these effects occurred without deliberate intention or awareness by the perceivers who were generally unaware of the facial expressions of the model and, when they did notice that the model was sometimes smiling, of the association between the model's facial expressions and their own product evaluations.

In this context it might be a little surprising that there are lots of ads with models that seem very hesitant to smile. To understand this strange peculiarity we should once again point to the power of gender differences. It's much easier to find an ad featuring a serious, non-smiling man than one featuring a non-smiling woman. While a smile has been traditionally seen as an obligatory expression for female models, an embodiment of the gender ideals of agreeableness and vulnerability, it is not the case for men , who should rather look unemotional and detached. These stereotypes not only shape the advertisements themselves, but also their perception. There are studies in which both male and female participants tend to rank male models displaying enjoyment smiles lower than males displaying weak smiles or not smiling at all.

But good ads often break our expectations. It's quite hard to grab somebody's attention presenting something perfectly predictable. An ad featuring a female model wearing a smile would likely convey an agreeable, non-threatening, and suitably feminine attitude. Conversely, when women do not smile for the camera, the result is an arresting image —one that violates our expectations. The removal of a friendly and agreeable gesture does not create a blank impression. We're left with an unmitigated stare, a daring provocation. Such a confrontational look has become a default expression in women's fashion magazines since the 1980s.

Foto Bigstock

The smile on the female's lips is usually taken for granted. When a woman smiles, that smile usually does not speak for itself, it's probably there to put us in a right mood. The male smile, on the other hand, might speak volumes. The advertisers seem to acknowledge this effect and incorporate male smiles when they want to convey a specific message. Smiles are often used to represent men of color so as to undercut the racist association of a potential threat or danger. Sometimes they are meant to promote a 'new masculinity'. The smiling man might be portrayed as helping his wife with laundry or taking care of children.

Children's smiles seem even more "invisible" than those expressed by women. Everybody expects a child to smile, at least in a photo, and most of the children pictured in ads are actually smiling. However, if we want to make a child's expression really meaningful we have to ask a child to stop grinning. And hold the expression for a couple of seconds…

This is especially true of boy models. Let's look at the ads for young men's hip-hop clothing. Here, child models are often posed in very adult-like ways and never smile. Since a smile is often read as a display of appeasement and submission, its absence can create a strong impression of dominance and authority. Not smiling for the camera symbolically endows the child not only with the power but also with sophistication of an adult. In this particular context they consciously mimic a "cool pose" that becomes the signature gesture of hip-hop music culture. This is hip-hop clothing, after all!

Another explanation for the more hesitant approach to smiling that is characteristic of contemporary advertising aesthetics is a significant change in approach. There was a time when a smile was a standard but quite unremarkable requisite for any advertiser wanting to attract customers and sell products. In the 1980s brands promised a thin veneer of success. 'Greed is good' was a motto of the era. It all changed in the next decade , when advertising became more reality focused and moved from being purely about our fantasies to a signpost of who we really are. While the new approach hasn't been embraced by all, the new aesthetic becomes more and more visible.

There's also a change regarding modeling standards, at least for more sophisticated products. It seems to be a gradual transition from a somewhat plastic expression of pure bliss to more nuanced and complex facial displays. A significant decrease in proportion of full smiles in favor of partial smiles for men and women has been observed. The partial smile that creates a more knowing and somewhat ironic look is becoming more and more common.

Moreover, it seems that people are well and truly over the fake happy world of advertising. Most recent research shows that ads depicting positive emotion might not be more effective than those depicting negative or ambivalent feelings. Those "darker ads" work especially well if the consumers are highly interested not only in a product but also in an ad itself. It shows that if they really are they tend to pay more attention to detail. Ads picturing shiny happy people work better on less interested consumers, but can turn off more sophisticated customers who prefer deeper emotional connection with the product. Apparently a happy grin is not always a winning strategy.

CHAPTER 5

Expression of Love

Two groups that exchange smiles most naturally and eagerly are mothers and infants, and lovers. In this chapter I will analyze smiling from three perspectives. First, we take a look at flirtation scenarios, and gender roles involved in flirting from the days when it was perceived as the indecent activity of fallen women and perfidious men until the present day, when it's all done unashamedly in public. In another section I will analyze smiling between men and women in stable relationships. We will compare the nonverbal repertoire of the happily married couples and the couple who are about to get divorce. Last but not least, I will present smiling in the context of early mother-child interaction and a formation of the loving bond.

Anatomy of the Flirtatious Smile

The first serious study of flirting was done in the 1960's by Irenäus Eibl-Eibesfeldt, a disciple of Konrad Lorenz, whose weakness for grinning dogs I mentioned in the first chapter. He discovered that women in dozens of cultures, from Far East to South America, engage in a fairly fixed repertoire of gestures to signal sexual availability and interest. These gestures included: the eyebrow flash (an exaggerated raising of the eyebrows of both eyes, followed by a rapid lowering), turning the head so that the side of the neck is bared, and the coy smile. The sequential flirting gesture was so distinctive that the Austrian scientist was convinced that it represented primal behaviors driven by the old parts of our brain.

This early research was focused on women's behavioral strategies, as if men were not capable of the flirtatious smile. The coy smile has been interpreted as one part of a whole sequence of signs that shows female vulnerability and submissiveness. These labels are now often criticized by others researchers who believe that certain behaviors are once misinterpreted as signifying either dominance or submission. They argue that the original labeling was quite arbitrary, and gestures such as baring the neck might not necessarily reflect submission – it may have a lot more to do with the fact that the neck is an erogenous zone.

Also, the female role in flirting has been recently reanalyzed and redefined. Research has shown that the cultural myth that the man is always the sexual aggressor, pressing himself on a reluctant woman, is nothing more than a male fantasy. In the real world, it is a woman who usually makes the first move. Since this move is usually very subtle – it may easily go unnoticed. Small wonder, that men have come to be seen as initiators in the courtship dance, while in fact they are typically summoned by the smiles and glances of women.

When the art of flirting was carefully studied in the natural habitat of hotel bars, dance clubs and cocktail lounges it became obvious that men are much more likely to approach a woman if she first made repeated eye contact followed by smiling. Apparently men need encouragement before they will approach a woman. It does not mean however, that it is a woman now who should be seen as dominant in contrast to what was concluded in the earlier studies. In fact, neither gender wholly dominates in a flirtation; the picture is much more complicated.

According to one theory when people get close to us, we become physiologically aroused. If we feel positive about this arousal – the person is attractive and likeable – we will get closer to them. If it is too much we will back off. People unconsciously signal "come closer" by making eye contact or smiling nicely. If another person begins to get too close, however, people unconsciously signal that they should "back up" by smiling less and looking away. It's not possible to force intimacy by smiling more, but it pays to look closely at what another person is signaling. If your date reduces eye contact and draws back, you may have assumed too much intimacy and should withdraw.

While busy with flirting two people negotiate the level of intimacy they find most comfortable. The more mutual gazing and smiling, the more touching, the higher the intimacy level. As I have explained in more detail in Chapter Three, the scripts of behavior are usually dictated by gender roles. Men might feel that their goal is to decrease the interpersonal distance and to heighten the level of intimacy in the shortest possible time. Women might feel that they should "guard their territory" as long as possible. The mutual attraction is a factor that interferes and makes the situation more exciting and unpredictable.

At this moment we may easily agree that the smile is not a submissive gesture, but more likely a powerful tool of social influence. It works both as a mark of sexual interest and sexual availability. There is also no doubt that the smile is an important part of the flirtation sequence, but is it really as coy as it was once portrayed? And should it be seen as an exclusively female strategic weapon? Actually, in the more recent discussions on smiling in a flirtation context it is a "flirter" of unspecified gender who smiles, and the former coy smile has been redefined as a flirtatious smile. In Paul Ekman's typology of smiles we find the following description:

> The flirter shows a felt smile while facing and gazing away from the person of interest and then, for a moment, steals a glance at the person, long enough to be just noticed as the glance shifts away again.

In my opinion, what is particularly fascinating about the flirtatious smile is its dynamic relation to other nonverbal gestures, especially the glance. In psychological research the smile has been typically isolated from the context; here it would be simply impossible. Smiles and glances not only build a meaningful dramatic sequence, but reinforce each other.

Unfortunately, Ekman didn't precisely define how long a proper flirtatious smile should last and what it is supposed to look like. He only suggested that we should consult the famous Mona Lisa picture for cues. At least we could happily agree that this is not a flashy grin. For more information we should consult those who study dating and courtship behavior. According to them the flirtatious smile is often described as a rather subtle half-smile with the teeth not displayed, or displayed only partially. Moreover, it was concluded that the smiles judged as the most flirtatious and trustworthy at the same time last just over half of a second. It seems like a very short moment, but even smiles that last 0.1 of a second are pretty noticeable. However, those brief smiles were judged much less favorably.

But shouldn't the flirtatious smile be as brief as possible? Let's have another look at what people actually do when they are flirting on a Saturday night out. Observational studies demonstrated that although brief coy smiles are present in the flirtation context, women as well as men tend to maintain direct eye contact for long periods and smiled fully and unabashedly. What's even more interesting, bold smiles outnumbered the coy ones.

The best way to solve this scientific embarrassment is to point to the fact that flirtation is not just a short sequence of nonverbal gestures. It is a complex interaction between two people. It may last minutes and be quickly terminated, but if the chemistry works well, it may last hours, be repeated over a certain period of time, and result in a more or less stable relationship. It means that if we're particularly interested in the dynamics of flirtatious smiling, it's essential to document flirtation from the very start. This scientific zeal may be diagnosed as voyeurism but it's certainly worth taking a risk. If we look close and for long enough, coy smiles should be more characteristic of the earliest stages, while the bolder and longer smiles are reserved for the stages when a relationship is already established and people are clearly enjoying themselves. It may seem obvious but such data is typically missing from psychological reports.

Another factor worth considering while analyzing flirtatious smiling is culture. Yes, it's culture again! The early comparative studies on flirtation demonstrated that what's striking here, are the cross-cultural similarities, not differences. Consequently it was rather biological, hard-wired programming than social learning which was emphasized as the main mechanism guiding human behavior. Today, researchers usually try to combine biological and cultural perspectives; however at least in the social sciences there seems to be much more of a focus on culture.

The cultural influences might manifest themselves in many different ways. For instance, cultures differ in the degree of freedom that is left for an unsupervised interaction between men and women. An exchange of glances between strangers, let alone flirtatious smiles, could be very suspicious. In many Muslim countries unmarried women are not expected to socialize freely with men other than family members. A smile from an unknown woman is typically seen as a sexual invitation. Since the early 1960s, American women who attended the American University in Beirut as exchange students have been told in the orientation programs not to smile at people they did not know personally, for smiling at strangers continually led to harassment.

Even in the more westernized Arab countries, like Egypt or Morocco, there are still regions where a flirtatious smile on a woman's face indicates her profession. Only prostitutes dare to smile that way. There are other places, like Saudi Arabia or Afghanistan, where women in public often hide their faces behind the veil, so even when they do smile, their smiles remain unnoticed.

This may look strange and oppressive, but it used to be quite similar in our comfortable Western world. At the end of the 19th century flirting was universally considered suspicious or even "disgraceful" activity for women as well as for men. While meeting a man for a date a single woman had to be accompanied by a chaperone, and a tight escort regime was advised even for engaged couples. It was generally assumed that the couple should never be left alone together until the wedding day. There was actually no place left for flirtation as we know it. Every smile and glance had to be subtle and discreet with no obvious sexual undertones.

Such an old-fashioned pattern of courtship has been preserved for a longer time in more conservative regions, elsewhere, in US or in Western Europe, gradual changes were introduced with flirting becoming more and more common and acceptable. However the gender roles proved quite rigid.

In South and Central America ideologies of *marianismo* and *machismo* prescribe strict gender roles. The ability to seduce women and have multiple sexual partners has been traditionally seen as one of the primary male virtues, while women who flirt openly, talk about sex, and act like they enjoy sex might be considered promiscuous and "lacking virtue". Modesty, faithfulness, and virginity represent feminine ideals. Consequently Latinas have been traditionally sorted into two categories of women. Flirtatious girls are sexually experienced and condemned, good girls remain virgins (*señoritas*) until marriage and never actively initiate sex. Although young women from Latin America or Americans of Hispanic heritage try to reject traditional roles and are less tolerant of machismo, gender stereotypes still exist.

In contrast, in the metropolises of Western Europe and the US, women's actual or pretended passivity is no longer seen as mandatory and coy smiles have been more and more often replaced by the bolder ones. Probably the first step towards sexual emancipation was the acceptance of lipstick which was used by women in their attempt to look seductive.

Although lipstick has a long history (for instance Cleopatra had her lipstick famously made from crushed beetles, which gave a deep red pigment), it was only in the late

1920s when it became popular on a mass scale. From now on it would be hard to imagine a flirtatious smile with no cosmetic enhancement. Another cosmetic invention helping women in their quest to look sexy and seductive was mascara, which was used to thicken and lengthen the eyelashes. The social changes following WWI brought a more relaxed attitude towards morals and cosmetics, although the transformation was not so smooth. As an author of a 1927 etiquette book put it:

> Oddly enough, even in modern times cosmetics still cause a lift of the eyebrows in some circles. Our old generation shudders at our younger generation's frank use of the lipstick. But that very frankness makes a lipstick virtuous! It is only an immoral motive which can make cosmetics iniquitous.

Today, almost half century after the Sexual Revolution, these words sound sweetly innocent.

Between Lovers

Sometimes flirting may lead to something as spectacular as a romantic relationship. Sometimes it is to the great surprise of both parties, and it takes good skills and courage to make it all work, long term. Nonverbal behaviors, which appear so essential in the courting stage, are also a primary way of creating intimacy in newly established relationships. Along with other nonverbal signals such as an open posture, gentle tone of voice, and gentle touch, smiling has been classified as a cue of 'intimacy' or interpersonal 'arousal' –expressions which serve to 'warm up' the affective quality of interaction.

It really works. Couples who are emotionally closer smile and laugh more than do couples who maintain a psychological distance. Not only do those who are happily married smile more often than unhappy couples, but they are more successful in using smiles in communication. For happily married men and women, smiling is both expected and well understood. It seems that they are really well-skilled at decoding each others' non-verbal messages.

If everything goes right, as relationships grow in intimacy, the partners match or synchronize nonverbal behaviors. This leads to trust in the relationship, as the predictability of the other's behavior brings security to the relationship. Happy couples often show synchronous expressions, so the husband and the wife would break into a smile or laugh in precisely the same moment.

But usually women smile more than their male partners or husbands. They also laugh more. In their relationships, women foster intimacy by smiling more often than men and giving their partners hugs or kisses when something nice happens. Married men often talk about their happiness but typically do not express their feelings. They have probably learnt not to be expressive of their underlying emotions.

According to some feminist writers, among women's most significant arduous tasks are in the form of emotional gestures, such as mandatory smiles and the faking of orgasms. It's like wives and husbands have signed a kind of 'emotional contract' in which the woman is expected to take care of emotional needs of her man. This is sort of emotional labor which could be compared to the everyday smiling routines of clerks and waitresses I described in the previous chapter. For some readers, especially the wives, who practice "household-smiling" on a daily basis, this may not sound very surprising, but what might come as a shock is the conventionality and striking rigidity of this type of arrangement. When we look through Victorian marriage guide books, we find that smiling was defined as "women's work". It was presented as a duty a wife owes to her husband, something she should practice and cultivate. A good wife should learn to "always wear a smile."

Many of our social routines changed during the 20th century: women may vote, work, and even flirt openly, but in romantic relationships gender roles proved to be surprisingly rigid. For sure, there is more equality than before, and there has been a shift from traditional marriage patterns towards companionate relationships, but when we look at *actual* behaviors the picture is not so rosy.

It's true that the emergent ideal of the companionate marriage, centered on sexual intimacy, personal fulfillment, mutual trust and love, has probably transformed the way young people perceive their stable relationship. It's also true that, unlike their parents, young couples are not primarily held together by mutual respect and the fulfillment of some gender specific obligations such as women's housework and motherhood, but when it comes to emotional management, gender roles are still clearly defined. Interestingly, the most common form of mismatch in contemporary American couples is that between an egalitarian woman and a 'transitional man' – that is, a man who pays lip-service to egalitarian values but remains traditional and conservative 'underneath'.

Gender differences manifest themselves also in the way men and women cope with their jealousy. In general, jealous men focus on their egos and try to re-establish their self-esteem, while jealous women are more likely to do something which might strengthen their relationship and save it from falling apart.

In one intriguing study, the couples who were invited to a laboratory were introduced to a young "assistant", a handsome man or a beautiful woman. During the experiment, the assistants began to openly flirt with one of the subjects. They even asked for the telephone number and on top of it wanted to meet later for a drink, completely ignoring the other person. Reacting to this obvious provocation, both men and women tried to ignore the flirting rivals seducing their partners, but while the men did little to mask their irritation, the jealous women kept smiling.

Despite the fact, that psychologists usually underscore the positive, affiliative qualities of smiling, suggesting that it is more likely to be manifested in situations in which people feel love, happiness, or attraction in the presence of others, they might also be present in a situation in which people feel hatred, disgust or contempt. Clinical psychologist, John Gottman, spent years studying the behavior of happy and distressed couples. He observed that in unhappy marriages, men and women both used the smile to express mutual contempt. Those were specifically cold, contemptuous sneers, which had been usually accompanied by frowns and rude gestures. Men, for instance often threw up their hands in disgust.

Gottman claims he can predict which couple will eventually divorce, and which will remain married after watching the couple for just five minutes. Usually he is really good in these predictions, boasting an astonishing 91 % accuracy. There are four types of negative interaction that are so lethal to a marriage that he has labeled them, accordingly, the "Four Horseman of the Apocalypse". These are Criticism, Contempt, Defensiveness, and Stonewalling.

Each of these deadly horsemen can be used to predict divorce by themselves, but typically they are found together in an unhappy marriage. Contempt is the worst of the four horsemen, because it communicates bad feelings directly to the person one is supposed to love. It's also impossible to solve a problem when the message being sent is that one partner is disgusted with the other. On a verbal level, Contempt comprises sarcasm, cynicism, name-calling, mockery and hostile humor. The nonverbal component is no less important, and contemptuous smiling (usually referred to as sneering) is the most characteristic signal. It seems then, that smiling might as well predict the stability of marriage as its quick dissolution; however it's hard to mistake a loving smile for a contemptuous sneer.

Motherly Love and the Bonding Smile

Some scientists have found that when two people are experiencing love they take on the expression that mothers often display when they are happily gazing at their infants. Their faces soften, and a slight, tender smile plays about their lips. A bond between a mother and her child is one of the most fascinating, especially in the earliest stages. The relationship between mothers and infants also proved to be critical for child development. In the early stages of attachment, babies use "social releasers", such as crying and smiling to elicit adults' caregiving. Smiling, in particular, may be considered an important part of the system that serves to establish a bond between the mother and the child.

During early infancy is an involuntary byproduct of the fluctuations in tension or arousal, it's not controlled or managed, but it soon becomes linked to familiar social stimuli. From about three months, smiling is truly social and reciprocal. This means that a baby's smiles are synchronized with those of the mother. However, smiles are not restricted to visual stimuli. By six weeks, babies smile in response to voices, particularly to the familiar sound of their mother's voice.

Psychologists always believed that adults are innately programmed to respond to these signals, which could be seen as ultimate and actually the only reward a mother gets for all

Photo Bigstock

the inconveniences and sacrifices crucial to nursing. Recent research using developed brain-scanning techniques confirms these assumptions.

First-time mothers with infants were put in a functional magnetic resonance imaging scanner and asked to look at photos of their own babies and other infants. In some of the photos which were presented to mothers, babies were smiling or happy. In others they were sad, and in some they had neutral expressions. It may sound technical, but actually, it's quite straightforward: when we look at the scans, areas of increased blood flow "light up," giving a clue as to where brain activity takes place. What scans showed was that the reward centers of mothers' brains were activated by their own child's facial expressions, but not by the faces of other children. The strongest activation was with smiling faces.

Interestingly, the areas stimulated by the sight of their own babies were those associated with the neurotransmitter dopamine. Similar activation patterns have been seen in response to pictures of romantic partners and sexual stimuli, suggesting a link between reward circuits and attachments. Moreover, these are the same areas that have been activated in experiments associated with drug addiction. It seems that seeing your own baby's smiling face is like a "natural high" very similar to the narcotic bliss we experience during the first stages of love.

CHAPTER 6

Putting Smiles into Context

When we think about talk and body gestures, we usually imagine nonverbal communication as a sort of speech supplement – something, which might be added before or after the sentence. Surely, it makes the whole conversation livelier and probably more enjoyable as well, but basically we can easily make the message work without these gestural ornaments. Words are the real message. Surprisingly, this lay approach greatly influenced the scientific assumptions about the mutual relationship between verbal and nonverbal messages. For years, nonverbal behavior has been completely absent from research in discourse analysis. Only relatively recently, scientists have started questioning this way of thinking.

Now it is kind of obvious that language and nonverbal messages work together and to fully understand the meaning of the so-called *utterance*, we should not ignore the nonverbal part. Moreover we should not separate verbal and nonverbal components since nonverbal behavior is inextricably bound to the verbal communication. Not only are they bound tightly, but they are also integrated simultaneously. It's rather uncommon to say something and then demonstrate it by facial expression or gestures. Typically, nonverbal communication is timed to occur precisely with the words that it is supposed to illustrate or supplement. Everything is perfectly synchronized. As Adam Kendon elegantly put it:

> At the same time, as the speaker packages meaning into phrases of speech, he or she is also packing meaning into phrases of gestures. Gesture phrases and tone units tend to match because they are being produced under the guidance of a single conceptual unit.

In the previous chapters, the smile has been somewhat isolated from the context of speech. This is still common practice not only in the research, but also in the theoretical thinking. Here I would like to put the smile back where it belongs: in the more general context of communication practices. It is difficult to imagine conversation devoid of any facial signals. People not only talk, but they raise their eyebrows, widen their eyes, they frown and smile. Oh, they do smile a lot!

Smiles in Conversation

Since smiles may have different meanings they can also be used in different ways in conversation. There have been some attempts to categorize conversational nonverbal signals, but while they might work well on a more general level, they're not always that handy when it comes to specific nonverbal acts, like smiling. Here, I would like to present my categorization of smiles used in conversations.

1. Illustrating the words

The term *illustrator* refers to the nonverbal behaviors that illustrate speech. Illustrators are closely related to words and usually they are meant to augment the verbal message. They also help to explain what is being said. It's quite interesting

Photo Bigstock

that illustrators are often taken for granted, and noticed only when they're strangely missing. Imagine your colleague saying he's glad to see you without a hint of a smile. It wouldn't seem too sincere, would it?

Smiles as illustrators may also serve a self-priming function: they have the power to command the listener's attention. Smiles can impress others as a sign of sociability and friendliness. Smiles are also heavily used by liars to mask their own uneasiness and embarrassment and provide the image of a reliable and relaxed person. Deception cues, however, can be identified in slow-motion video records. What such records reveal are so called *micro expressions.*

According to Paul Ekman, a micro expression is a complete emotional expression that is compressed in time. Typically it lasts only one-twenty-fifth of second, and then it is covered quickly by another expression. For example, a defendant might get scared that she's started losing the plot while presenting her elaborate fictional account of events and consequently displays a micro expression of fear. This might be quickly followed by a seemingly relaxed smile – a cover for the initial fear.

2. Ameliorating

One of the functions of smiling is the amelioration of a negative message carried by the words. The smile should be genuine, or at least should appear so. A Duchenne smile adds warmth, comfort and empathy so we can easier swallow an emotionally challenging message. A negative message usually concerns the listener. Sometimes it is the speaker who tries to offset the negative information concerning his or herself, pretending that it's not such a "big deal" anyway. This might be purely egocentric ('See, I am so cool'), or allocentric (i.e. focused on others well-being), when someone wants to spare others the worry.

The negative content of the verbal message may vary from relatively unimportant events like failing an exam to much more serious ones like terminal illness, or losing a relative. While in the former cases a nice smile does the job well, in others it is usually accompanied by words and other nonverbal expressions emphasizing our compassion.

Generally we should expect more ameliorating smiles within family and close personal relationships. In some contexts, like doctor-patient relationship, psychotherapy or counseling, compassionate smiles might be part of standard procedures, especially while dealing with serious illness.

There might also be cross-cultural differences in the preference for amelioration in various social contexts. The more we value harmony, the more we are concerned with another's well-being, and the more smiles we use to soften or sweeten the messages which might potentially hurt somebody.

In my comparative analysis of smiling in Polish and American movies praised for their psychological realism, I found a significant difference in the use of the ameliorating smile, with the Americans using this type of smile much more frequently. Generally, there were almost twice as many incidences of smiling in the American movies. Moreover, while in the American films the higher frequency of smiling was typically associated with positive characters, in Polish movies it was the villains who smiled most often. Apparently, smiling is still considered a suspicious activity in Poland, something which is closer associated with manipulation than with kindness.

3. Commenting

In the case of illustrating and amelioration, we invariably use the smile as a positive nonverbal signal. In the case of nonverbal *comments*, the smile might have a positive value, but it might also be used to mock somebody's idea they are currently presenting, or to express our contempt.

Comments can be personal reactions to something that happened in the past. A person could smile ironically, commenting on the naivety of his colleague who makes unsafe transactions on the Internet. Other personal reactions can be evaluations about what is just being said or what is just taking place.

Smiles may also convey information about reactions to events which are anticipated in the future. A young woman might smile while describing details of her planned wedding reception to her best friend. Someone else may grin devilishly explaining his plan to humiliate the long-time enemy.

4. Contradicting the words

This is probably the most interesting example of the tight bond between verbal and nonverbal communication. The statement 'I hate you' said with a particular intonation and with the smile changes the underlying meaning dramatically. Of course, the same is true of 'I love you, honey' declared with the sneer of contempt.

Contradiction could be a good vehicle for making jokes, but could be also used in order to humiliate or embarrass somebody. "Oh my, what a funky shirt!" – could be a sincere complement, but together with the ironic smile it could instead be an insult.

However, the interpretation of the contradictory messages might be quite complicated. In one recent study researchers tested the effects of smiles in conjunction with statements conveying disgust and anger. Interestingly while the smiles had the power to completely change the negativity of the verbal message in context of disgust (e.g., "I went to visit my granddad the other day. He spits when he talks and he managed to sneeze all over my face."), their impact was much subtle in the context of anger (e.g., "My boss decided to promote his son to a position he knew I wanted. He knows I worked much harder and better than his son."). As authors point out: "we may react positively to jokes that involve verbal expressions of disgust that are accompanied by smiles. However, if a verbal statement conveys anger rather than disgust, exactly the same smiles might evoke a less positive reaction".

A contradiction might be intended and obvious, but quite often we're not conscious about discrepancies between how we act and what we say. A term *double bind* refers to the situation in which two messages are contradictory. The contradiction may be unexpressed in its immediate context and therefore implicit and invisible. A double bind typically includes explicit verbal communication being contradicted by implicit nonverbal signs. The classic example of a negative double bind is of a mother telling her child 'I love you' while at the same time turning her head away in disgust. The child doesn't know how to respond to the conflict between the words and the nonverbal message and is trapped in a dilemma. Such destructive double binds are a frequent pattern of communication among families of schizophrenic patients.

5. Supporting requests

Some time ago two curious German psychologists tried to investigate the status of the nonverbal component when people ask for a small favor. They concluded that people use the smile differently. Some smiled during the second half of the utterance, some during the whole utterance, but there were many that did not smile at all. They concluded that interrogative intonation seems to be the crucial nonverbal element in this context, and smiling was not as important as they expected. However, the results might have been different had the experiments been carried out in the cultural context of America. In Germany, people tend to use the smile quite hesitantly outside of their close personal circle. In the research under discussion, the situation was quite formal: asking a secretary to make a coffee.

6. Feedback

Here, for the first time, we focus not on the speaker's behavior but on the listener.

Along with head nods and statements such as 'uh-huh' or 'yeah', smiling has its separate function as the so-called *back-channel*. Backchannels are the sounds or gestures made in conversation by the listener, which grease the wheels of conversation. The backchannels could be categorized into five groups:

1) Continuers (when the listener encourages the speaker to finish the idea being conveyed).
2) Requests for clarification.
3) Displays of agreement.
4) Displays of understanding.
5) Displays of emotional response.

Smiles can provide feedback on three levels: they indicate a positive personal reaction (often merely polite), as well as understanding of and participation in the conversation. Although backchanneling seems to be a universal phenomenon, specific types and functions of the backchannels might differ from one speech community to another. It seems that American conversational routines tend to be guided by a friendliness principle, thus the backchannels are typically utilized to convey agreement and understanding. Of course, not all Americans are so agreeable, and there are important gender differences (with women being usually more agreeable, and smiling than men), but there's clearly a pattern here – a model for a good, friendly conversation.

A distinctiveness of the French conversational style from American standards has been supported empirically. Research shows that arguing affirms closeness between the speakers, and shows that their relationship can withstand differing opinions. Moreover, the French interactional style encourages contribution to the conversation while the interlocutor is still speaking. This overlapping shows that one is so interested and involved (*engagé*) in the conversation, that one cannot wait until the end of the interlocutor's turn before contributing. Similar rules operate in Germany, Poland, and Russia, where an agreeable attitude and the use of smiling as a backchannel is generally not encouraged, especially in more informal conversations.

Facial Dialogues

In the Western world we usually assume that the words constitute the main part of a message. Even if we know the importance of nonverbal signals, what we usually do to make ourselves clear is try to find the right words to express what we feel or think. Interestingly, there are cultures in which people have quite different ideas about good communication.

In his book, *Beyond Culture*, Edward Hall introduced an important dimension of culture: high versus low context. According to Hall, low context cultures are those in which most information is transmitted in a relatively direct fashion through language. In contrast, in high context cultures, the meaning is implicit, contained in the situation and the subtle nonverbal acts of individuals. Consequently people usually have no choice but to "read between the lines" to appreciate the true meaning of what somebody says. In high context cultures, the receivers of messages attend closely to the nonverbal channel in relating to others. In effect, receivers bear a greater responsibility for understanding nonverbal messages in high context interactions than receivers do in low context interactions.

High-context cultures thrive in the Far East. Two philosophical traditions, Buddhism and Confucianism, helped to establish the specific patterns of communication observed in Japan, Korea, and China. It is generally assumed that communication through words is much less reliable than heart-to-heart communication through an intuitive grasp of things.

One of the most important ideals in Japanese society is *omoiyari*. *Omoiyari* could be roughly translated as 'empathy', but it's more than that. Some researchers define it as a unique ability to read other people's minds and a willingness to respond to their needs. In her insightful psychological study of Japanese culture, Takie Sugiyama Lebra emphasizes the importance of *omoiyari* in the context of Japanese culture. She comments:

> The Japanese glorify silent communication, *ishin denshin* ('heart to heart communication'), and mutual 'vibrations', implying the possibility of semi-telepathic communication. Words are paltry against the significance of reading subtle signs and signals and the intuitive grasp of each other's feelings.

As you might guess, there is no specific Japanese gene responsible for *omoiyari*. Such ability is only possible as a result of intensive cultural training. So-called "omoiyari training" has a prominent place in the socialization of Japanese children. From an early age, they are taught by their mothers to read other people's minds and understand another's perspective. A common game is to ask children to attribute speech to people who had not actually spoken – e.g. 'You see that your older sister is upset. What do you think she would say if she addressed you now?' *Omoiyari* education is also an important part of the school curriculum.

But guessing what one feels or thinks is a very tricky business. And even more so in the East. According to Confucian principles the emotions should be concealed at all times, and the face should be no more than a polite mask. Consequently, smiling in East Asia typically represents courtesy or is used in order to conceal 'bad' feelings, like embarrassment or irritation, which might disrupt social harmony –something which is valued the most highly. I have already mentioned this in Chapter Two, describing the importance of *wa* in Japanese culture.

Similar cultural norms operate in Indonesia. Indonesians, either from Bali, Java, or Sulawesi, smile effortlessly as they meet people, speak with others, or encounter experiences that are neither funny, nor delightful. For these reasons, many first-time visitors to Indonesia have been misled to think that Indonesians are always happy and hospitable. However, this may lead to far more serious misunderstandings, as in the case of media coverage of the trial of the Indonesian terrorist Amrozi, who was responsible for the bombing in Bali in October 2002. Amrozi, who soon gained international notoriety as "The Smiling Bomber", indeed smiled quite often during the whole trial and his smiles were almost unequivocally interpreted as an ostentatious display of arrogance and a lack of remorse.

However in high context cultures, smiles could have also other meanings and their interpretation is a difficult skill which could hardly be learned by a foreigner. Let's focus on the legendary Thai smile as an example. That smile –called "yim" in Thai – is perceived as being just about the most appropriate "answer" to any possible situation. It's used to show happiness, embarrassment, fear, tension, resignation and remorse. For foreigners, these smiles all look the same, but for Thais their smiles offer an amazing array of shadows and tones. Here is just a small selection of Thai smiles, the tip of the iceberg:

yim tak tai: The polite smile, used for strangers
yim cheuat cheuan: The winner's smile over a rival
yim tang nam dtah: The happy smile
yim hairng: The nervous, apologetic smile
yim sao: The smile masking sadness or unhappiness
yim mee lay-nai: The evil smile
yim cheun chom: The smile of admiration
yim yor: The arrogant smile
yim mai ork: The forced smile

The true meanings of these seemingly identical expressions could only be guessed contextually. A slightly higher pitch of the voice, stiff posture or smiling eyes would be very helpful tips. Thais understand the realities behind a smile immediately and act accordingly while Westerners need confirmation by words. However, Thais may say "yes" and smile, but every Thai knows what is really meant: "No", "Maybe", or, perhaps, "Not yet sure."

Interestingly, this focus on contextual aspects of communication influenced the way Asian people deal with answering machines. Answering machines are quite useful communication devices, but there is one little problem –they deprive the speaker of any backchannel responses from the recipient of the message. No smiles, no frowns, no changes in a voice's pitch. Nothing, just silence.

You might imagine that for someone who relies strongly on the contextual aspects of communication, leaving a message on an answering machine presents a demanding and quite frustrating task. In one cross-cultural study the majority of Japanese participants complained about the lack of a typical relational bond between the speaker and the listener (e.g. "It is hard to speak because there are no responses.", "I cannot tell the reaction of the receiver."), which was not seen as a problem by the Americans. Moreover, it was found out that Japanese callers use their answering machines less often than American callers, and are more likely to hang up when they reach one. When Japanese participants left a message under laboratory conditions, they were more sensitive to the nature of the relationship as indicated in their more pronounced message tailoring. Small wonder that answering machines manufactured in Japan offer a longer time limit for each incoming message than those made by American companies.

Invasion of the Smiley Faces

Smiles not only supplement and complement spoken language; they are also present in the written language, especially in the context of internet communication. The idea of a smiling face as a typographical sign is often traced back to 1969. In his *New York Times* interview, the famous writer, Vladimir Nabokov, widely known for his once scandalous novel Lolita, was asked how he ranks himself among living novelists – a question that apparently he did not find terribly clever. He answered it anyway:

> I often think there should exist a special typographical sign for a smile — some sort of concave mark, a supine round bracket, which I would now like to trace in reply to your question.

In today's technology enhanced world, computer-mediated communication (often referred to as CMC) is an important part of life for many; not only in the Western world, but almost everywhere. In 2006 only 1 in 25 people in Africa was an Internet user, compared with a world average of 1 in 6, and more than 1 in 3 for Europe, but there is a clear trend for ever-greater availability. The Internet use growth in Africa in the next few years has been estimated to be 625.8%.

Of the various media of CMC, e-mail is the most popular. Although, the usage of e-mail outweighs any other medium, including face to face communication and telephone, e-mail still has limitations of its own. In e-mails, text is the main method of conveying a message, so it lacks the typical non-verbal cues of human communication. Hence, the invention of emoticons – non-verbal cues to supplement the meaning of textual verbal messages. The word "emoticon" is a term coined from "emotion" and "icon". As the name indicates, emoticons were introduced to communicate facial expressions or body gestures when expressing opinions or moods online.

The most widely used emoticon is the "smiley face", which represents the sentiment that the sender is pleased and happy. More recent software, such as instant messengers, provides graphic emoticons: small images that automatically replace typed combinations of certain characters; the users may select them from a menu. By supplementing the verbal message, emoticons can help emphasize the intended mood of the message. This is especially useful when a message is intended as humorous, sarcastic or ironic.

Research shows that emoticons actually have an influence on the impressions formed of the sender's character or attitude. For example, chat room moderators who used emoticons were perceived to be more "dynamic," "friendlier," and more "talkative" compared to those moderators who did not use emoticons. Others found that an e-mail message with emoticons resulted in a more favorable impression towards the sender compared to an e-mail with no emoticons. However, it seems that the usage of emoticons becomes more habitual over time. Emoticons may function as ritualized expressions such as 'How do you do?' that are exchanged not to convey particular meaning but because we are trained to be nice.

Despite the claim that CMC neutralizes distinctions of gender, women and men exhibit different styles and they value different kinds of online interactions as appropriate and desirable. In one recent study the use of emoticons on the Internet in same- and mixed-gender newsgroups was carefully analysed. The majority of emoticon use by females in same-gender newsgroups came under the category of humor, while the bulk of male emoticon use in predominantly male newsgroups expressed teasing or sarcasm. Moreover, her data show that males use more emoticons denoting teasing/sarcasm and humor on the (predominantly) same-gender newsgroup than in the mixed-gender newsgroups. Conversely, the female use of emoticons to express teasing or sarcasm and humor increased when moving from same-gender to mixed-gender newsgroups. These findings suggest that both genders converge toward each other on mixed-gender newsgroups. Even more striking is the finding that in mixed-gender groups, rather than the females adopting the *offline* male standard of less emotional expression, the opposite occurs: there are males who display an increase in emoticon use.

As you might have already guessed there are also cross-cultural differences in emoticon use. We tend to think of emoticons as a global and universal phenomenon. Actually, it is global but not really universal. Traditionally, the emoticon in Western style is written from left to right, the way one reads and writes in most Western cultures. Thus, most commonly, emoticons have the eyes on the left, followed by the nose and mouth. Users from East Asia popularized a style of emoticons that can be understood without tilting one's head to the left. But there are also other, more exciting differences.

In the United States and in the rest of the Western world the emoticon :-) symbolizes a happy face, whereas the emoticon :- (denotes a sad face. However, the Japanese tend to use the symbol (^_^) to indicate a happy face, and (; _ ;) to indicate sadness. Similar patterns are used by Koreans. Japanese and Korean emoticons for happiness and sadness vary in terms of how the eyes are depicted while Western emoticons vary the direction of the mouth.

It's more than just a graphic convention. The recent Japanese study shows that the Japanese emoticons reflect the way Japanese people tend to detect emotions in others. They rather look to the eyes for emotional cues, whereas Americans focus on the mouth region. The Japanese way seems more effective because the eyes are more difficult to control than the mouth so they probably provide better clues about a person's emotional state. Even the most pleasant smile may be just a mask that conceals what one really feels, but the eyes –they tell the truth! Surprised? This is exactly what Duchenne de Boulogne once demonstrated. In Asia they knew it from the start.

Epilogue

Throughout this book I tried to present the smile as a part of communication process. Not only in the face to face interaction but also in our virtual encounters on the net. It seems that whenever we smile we do it on purpose. Miles L. Patterson in his functional approach to nonverbal communication lists seven basic purposes that may be served by interactive behavior:

1) Providing information.
2) Regulating interaction.
3) Expressing intimacy.
4) Managing affect.
5) Exercising social control.
6) Presenting identities or images.
7) Facilitating service and task goals.

I hope I succeed in demonstrating how well this framework works for the smile. The smile may provide information about our positive attitude or mood, it also regulates interaction. We smile to express love and to foster intimacy while we flirt. Sometimes we try to look cheerful when we're not or smile to hide our irritation, thus managing our emotions. Smile is also associated with exercising social control, for instance we can smile signaling interest in meeting someone or ingratiating the person to gain support. In a similar vein we use smile in self-presentation to appear likeable or assertive. Finally smiles facilitate professional service encounters and may be seen as crucial element defining employee's model behavior. Frankly speaking, this variety of functions might be quite overwhelming! But the picture is even more complex. While writing on the smile in different social context I numerously pointed to the differences between various types of smiling. As Paul Ekman once remarked:

> "...Smiles should no longer be considered a single category of behavior. They can be usefully distinguished measuring different facets of the smile. It remains to be determined how many different smiles may provide different social signals, have different functions in social interaction and relate to different aspects of subjective experience".

It might have sounded bit controversial back then in 1988, but now it's something one cannot deny. The recent research is mostly focused on Duchenne smiles contrasting them with the false or posed smiles. This simple distinction has been repeatedly criticized but somehow works well in psychological laboratories. You might remember some examples from the book, for instance a study showing how smiling models may influence our choice of favorite T-shirt. Apparently people have quite precise ideas how genuine smiles should look, but perhaps it's time to go beyond Duchenne smile. There are so many other fascinating smiles still to be researched!

Another important point I tried to address in this book is the importance of context on smile's meaning and interpretation. Smiling usually takes place in a social space and is somehow mediated by it. The context may influence our judgment about the smiling person, their skills or personality. It also influences our judgments about genuineness of the smiles. Obviously the smile displayed by the car dealer will be interpreted as less genuine than a smile displayed by the person who's been just decorated with the gold Olympic medal. Another important factor is culture and here our practical knowledge often fails us. The world is shrinking fast, but as I tried to demonstrate in almost every chapter, the cultural smile codes are quite immune to the forces of globalization.

While researching the fascinating subject of smiling I accidentally came upon a lovely anecdote by an American professor. One day she was checking the test paper of an African student from Burkina Faso. Wishing to indicate her appreciation of a witty answer he had given to a question, she hurriedly sketched a little smiley face in the margin of his paper. When she returned the paper, the student came to her after class and was obviously angry. He pointed to the smiley face and said, 'Why do you think that?' He explained that he had felt deeply insulted when he saw it because in his country a smiley face would symbolize a silly person. As I have told you throughout this little book, smiling is a complex matter.

REFERENCES

Introduction

Darwin, E. (1801). *Zoonomia, or the Laws of Organic Life* (3rd ed. vol. 1, p. 206). London: J. Johnson

Hess, U., Baupré, M., & Cheung, N. (2002). Who to whom and why –cultural differences and similarities in the function of smiles. In M. Abel (Ed.), *An empirical reflection on the smile* (pp. 187–216). New York: The Edwin Mellen Press.

Niedenthal, P. M. & Maringer, M. (2009). Embodied emotion considered. *Emotion Review, 1*, 122-128.

Chapter 1

Caron, J. E. (2002). From ethology to aesthetics: Evolution as a theoretical paradigm for research on laughter, humor, and other comic phenomena. *Humor, 15*, 245–281.

Chevalier-Skolnikoff, S. (1982). A cognitive analysis of facial behaviour in Old World monkeys, apes, and human beings. In C. T. Snowden, C. H. Brown, M.R. Peterson (Eds.), *Primate communication* (pp. 303–368). Cambridge: Cambridge University Press.

Fridlund, A. (1994). *Human facial expression: An evolutionary view.* New York: Academic Press.

Owren, M. J., Bachorowski, J. (2001). The evolution of emotion expression: A selfish gene account of smiling in early hominids and humans. In T. J. Mayne, G. A. Bonanno (Eds.), *Emotions: Current issues and future directions* (pp. 152–191). New York: Guilford Press.

Porteous, J. (1989). Humor and social life. *Philosophy East and West: A Quarterly Journal of Asian and Contemporary Thought, 39*, 270-288.

Preuschoft, S. (2000). Primate faces and facial expressions. *Social Research, 67*, 245–270.

Schmidt, K. L. & Cohn, J. F. (2001). Human facial expressions as adaptations: Evolutionary questions in facial expression research.*Yearbook of Physical Anthropology, 44*, 3-24.

Van Hoof, J. A. (1972). A comparative approach to the phylogeny of laughter and smiles. In R. A. Hinde (Ed.), *Non-verbal communication* (pp. 209–241). Cambridge: Cambridge University Press.

Chapter 2

Akiyama, K. (1991). A comparative study of facial expressions and emblems between Japanese and Americans. *Intercultural Communication Studies, 1*, 147-164.

Brown, W.M., Palameta, B., Moore, C. (2003). Are there nonverbal cues to commitment? An exploratory study using the zero-acquaintance video presentation paradigm. *Evolutionary Psychology, 1*, 42-69.

Chen, B. (2006). Cultural differences in smiling. *US-China Foreign Language, 4*, 15-18.

Duchenne de Boulogne, G.-B. (1862/1990). *The mechanisms of human facial expression.* Cambridge: Cambridge University Press.

Frank, M. G., Ekman, P., & Friesen, W. V. (1993). Behavioral markers and recognizability of the smile of enjoyment. *Journal of Personality and Social Psychology, 64*, 83-93.

Godoy, R., Reyes-Garcia, V., Huanca, T., Tanner, S., Leonard, W.R., McDade, T., Vadez, V. (2005). Do smiles have a face value? Panel evidence from Amazonian Indians. *Journal of Economic Psychology, 26*, 469-490.

Patterson, M. L., Iizuka, Y., Tubbs, M. E., Ansel, J., Tsutsumi, M., & Anson, J. (2007). Passing encounters east and west: Comparing Japanese and American pedestrian interactions. *Journal of Nonverbal Behavior, 31,* 155-166.

Scharlemann, J. P. W., Eckel, C. C., Kacelnik, A., Wilson, R. K. (2001). The value of a smile: Game theory with a human face. *Journal of Economic Psychology, 22*, 617–640.

Stephenson, S. (2003). *Understanding Spanish-Speaking South Americans.* Yarmouth, Maine: Intercultural Press.

Stewart, E. C., Bennett, M. J. (1991). *American Cultural Patterns: A Cross-Cultural Perspective.* Yarmouth, Maine: Intercultural Press.

Terzani, T. (1997). *A Fortune-Teller Told Me: Earthbound Travels in the Far East.* London: HarperCollins.

Triandis, H. C., Marín, G., Lisansky, J., & Betancourt, H. (1984). Simpatía as a cultural script of Hispanics. *Journal of Personality and Social Psychology, 47*, 1363-1375.

Wierzbicka, A. (1997). *Cultures through their key words: English, Russian, Polish, German, and Japanese.* New York: Oxford University Press.

Ye, Z. (2006). Why the 'inscrutable' Chinese face? Emotionality and facial expression in Chinese, In C. Goddard (Ed.), *Ethnopragmatics: Understanding Discorse in Cultural Context* (pp. 127-169). Berlin-New York: Mouton de Gruyter.

Chapter 3

Baudrilliard, J. (1989). *America* (translated by Chris Turner). New York: Verso. Carnegie, D. B. (1936). *How to Win Friends and Influence People.* New York: Simon & Schuster.

Goffman, E. (1959). *The Presentattion of Self in Everyday Life.* New York: Anchor Books.

Handley, P.M. (2006). *The King Never Smiles: A Biography of Thailand's Bhumibol Adulyadej.* New Haven: Yale University Press.

Jones, E.E., & Pittman, T.S. (1982). Toward a general theory of strategic self-presentation. In J. Suls (Ed.), *Psychological perspectives of the self* (pp. 231-261). Hillsdale, NJ: Erlbaum.

Khuri, F. (2007). *An Invitation to Laughter: A Lebanese Anthropologist in the Arab World.* Chicago: Chicago University Press.

Kotchemidova, C., From good cheer to „Drive-by smiling": A social history of cheerfulness. *Journal of Social History*, 2005, 39, 5-37.

Liden, R.C., Martin, C.L., & Parsons, C.K. (1993). Interviewer and applicant behaviors in employment interviews. *Academy of management Journal, 36*, 372-386.
Schroeder, F. (1998). Say cheese! The revolution in the aesthetics of smiles, *Journal of Popular Culture, 32*, 103–145.
Szarota, P. (2006). *Psychology of the Smile: A Cultural Analysis.* Gdansk: Gdanskie Wydawnictwo Psychologiczne (in Polish)
Szarota, P. (2010). The mystery of the European smile. *Journal of Nonverbal Behavior, 34,* 249-256.
Trumble, A. (2004). *A Brief History of the Smile.* New York: Basic Books.
Vrugt, A., Van Eechoud, M. (2002). Smiling and self-presentation of men and women for job photographs. *European Journal of Social Psychology, 32*, 419–431.
Wierzbicka, A. (1994). Emotion, language, and 'cultural scripts', In S. Kitayama & H. Markus (Eds.), *Emotion and Culture: Empirical Studies of Mutual Influence* (pp. 130-196), Washington: American Psychological Association.
Woodzicka, J. A. (2008). Sex differences in self-awareness of smiling during a mock job interview. *Journal of Nonverbal Behavior, 32*, 109-121.

Chapter 4

Bailey, B. (2000). Communicative behaviour and conflict between African-American customers and Korean immigrant retailers in Los Angeles. *Discourse & Society, 11*, 86-108.
Barger, P. B. & Grandey, A.A (2006). Service with a smile and encounter satisfaction: Emotional contagion and appraisal mechanisms. *Academy of Management Journal, 49*, 1229-1238.
Boulton, C. (2007). Don't smile for the camera: Black power, para-proxemics and prolepsis in print ads for hip-hop clothing. *International Journal of Communication, 1*, 758-788.
Carnegie, D. B. (1936). *How to Win Friends and Influence People.* New York: Simon & Schuster.

Drahota, A., Costall, A., & Reddy, V. (2007). The vocal communication of different kinds of smile. *Speech Communication, 50*, 278-287.

Endy, C. (2003). *Cold War Holidays: American Tourism in France*. Chapel Hill: University of North Carolina Press.

Fernandez-Dols, J., Carrera, P., Casado, C. (2002). The meaning of expression. Views from art and other sources. In L. Anolli & R. Ciceri (Eds), *Say not to say: New perspectives on miscommunication* (pp. 117–132). Amsterdam: IOS Press.

Fowler, J. & Christakis, N. (2009). Dynamic spread of happiness in a large social network. *British Medical Journal, 337*, 2249-58.

Hennig-Thurau, T., Groth, M., Paul, M., & Gremler, D.D. (2006). Are all smiles created equal? How emotional contagion and emotional labor affect service relationships, *Journal of Marketing, 70*, 58-73.

Hochschild, A. R. (1983). *The Managed Heart: Commercialization of Human Feeling.* Berkeley: University of California Press.

Lau-Gesk, L., & Meyers-Levy, J. (2009). Emotional persuasion: When the valence versus the resource demands of emotions influence customers' attitudes. *Journal of Consumer Research, 36*, 585-599.

Lewis, L. (2008). Smiling can seriously damage your health. *The Times*, February, 9

Muir, C. (2008). Smiling with customers. *Business Communication Quarterly, 71*, 241-246.

Peace, V., Miles, L, & Johnston, L. (2006). It doesn't matter what you wear. The impact of posed and genuine expressions of happiness on product evaluation. *Social Cognition, 24,* 137-168.

Pugh, S. D. (2001). Service with a smile: Emotional contagion in the service encounter. *Academy of Management Journal, 44*, 1018-1027.

Reitman, V. (1999). Learning to grin – and bear it. *Los Angeles Times,* February, 22

Strasser, S. (1993). The smile that pays: The culture of traveling salesman, 1880–1920. In J. Gilbert (Ed.), *The mythmaking frame of mind: Social imagination and American culture* (pp. 155–177). Belmont, CA: Wadsworth.

Watson, J.L. (2006). McDonald's in Hong Kong: Consumerism, dietary change, and the rise of a children culture, In J.L. Watson (Ed.) *Golden Arches East: McDonald's in East Asia* (pp. 77-110). Stanford: Stanford University Press.

Chapter 5

Bowlby, J. (1982). *Attachment and Loss* (vol.1). New York: Basic Books.

Ekman, P. (1985). *Telling Lies. Clues to Deceit in the Marketplace, Politics, and Marriage.* New York: W.W. Norton & Company.

Eibl-Eibesfeldt, I. (1989). *Human Ethology*. Piscataway, NJ: Aldine Transaction.

Faulkner, S. (2003). Good girl or flirt girl: Latinas' definitions of sex and sexual relationships. *Hispanic Journal of Behavioral Sciences, 25*, 177-200.

Gottman, J. M. (1994). *What Predicts Divorce?* Englewood Cliffs, NJ: Erlbaum.

Gueguen, N. (2008). The effect of a women's smile on men's courtship behavior. *Social Behavior and Personality, 36*, 1233-1236.

Krumhuber, E., Manstead, A. S.R., & Kappas, A. (2007). Facial dynamics as indicators of trustworthiness and cooperative behavior. *Emotion, 7*, 730-735.

Le Poire, B. A., & Strzyzewski, K. (1992). *Gender differences in the nonverbal expression of jealousy.* Tempe, AZ: University of Arizona.

Moore, M. M. (2010). Human nonverbal courtship behavior – A brief history review. *Journal of Sex Research, 47*, 171-180.

Sroufe, L., Waters, E. (1976). The ontogenesis of smiling and laughter; A perspective on the organization of development in infancy. *Psychological Review, 83,* 173–189.

Strathearn, L., Li, J., Fonagy, P, Read Montague, P. (2008). What's in a smile? Maternal brain responses to infant cues. *Pediatrics, 122*, 40-51.

Chapter 6

BangkokDan (2007). *The Thai smile.* Retrieved from absolutelybangkok.com on March 12, 2010

Brunner, L. J. (1979). Smiles can be back channels. *Journal of Personality and Social Psychology, 37*, 728-734.

Ekman, P., Friesen, W. (1969). The repertoire of nonverbal behaviour: Categories, origins, usage and coding. *Semiotica, 1,* 49–98.

Grabowski-Gellert, J., Winterhoff-Spurk, P. (1988). Your smile is my command: Interaction between verbal and nonverbal components of requesting specific to situational characteristics. *Journal of Language and Social Psychology, 7*, 229–242.

Kendon, A. (1981). *Nonverbal communication, interaction, and gesture.* New York: Mouton.

Krumhuber, E. & Manstead, A.S.R. (2009). Are you joking? The moderating role of smiles in the perception of verbal statements. *Cognition and Emotion, 23*, 1504-1515.

Szarota, P. (2007). The Japanese smile: Orientalist stereotype or cultural script? *Lud, 91*, 137-155 [in Polish].

Szarota, P, Bedyńska, S., Matsumoto, D., Yoo, S.H., Friedlmeier, W. et al. (2009). Smiling as a masking display strategy. Cross-cultural comparison. In A. Przepiórka & A. Błachnio (Eds.) *Closer to Emotions III* (pp. 227-238). Lublin: Wydawnictwo KUL

Wagner, H. L., Lee, V. (1998). Facial behaviour alone and in the presence of others. In P. Philippot, R. S. Feldman, & E. J. Coats (Eds.), *The social context of nonverbal behaviour* (pp. 262-286). Cambridge: Cambridge University Press.

Walther, J. B., & D'Addario, K. P. (2001). The impacts of emoticons on message interpretation in computer-mediated communication. *Social Science Computer Review, 19*, 324- 347.

Wolf, A. (2000). Emotional expressions online: Gender differences in emoticon use. *Cyber Psychology & Behavior, 3*, 827-833.

Yoo, J. H. (2007). To smile or not to smile: Defining the effects of emoticons on relational outcomes. Paper presented at the annual meeting of the International Communication Association, San Francisco, May, 24th.

Yuki, M., Maddux, W. W., & Masuda, T. (2007). Are the windows to the soul the same in the East and West? Cultural differences in using the eyes and mouth as cues to recognize emotions in Japan and the United States. *Journal of Experimental Social Psychology, 43*, 303-311.

Epilogue

Ekman, P, Friesen, W. V., & O'Sullivan, M. (1988). Smiles when lying. *Journal of Personality and Social Psychology, 54*, 414-420.

Patterson, M. L. (1991). A functional approach to nonverbal exchange. In R. S. Feldman & B. Rime (Eds.), *Fundamentals of nonverbal behavior.* Cambridge: Cambridge University Press.

FURTHER RECOMMENDED SOURCES

Abel, M. (2002). *An Empirical Reflection on the Smile.* New York: The Edwin Mellen Press.

This is the one and only academic study focused solely on smiling. It presents contemporary theories of smiling, and most popular research topics, e.g. gender differences in smiling, smiling in children, smiling and well-being. There is also a chapter on cultural differences in smiling.

Cole, J. & Spalding, H. (2009). *The Invisible Smile: Living without face expression.* New York: Oxford University Press.

Möbius Syndrome is a rare condition that deprives its victims of something we all take for granted. People with Möbius cannot smile, frown, or look surprised. This fascinating book presents life stories of people with this neurological condition and the varied ways in which they cope and adapt.

Ekman, P. (2007). *Emotions Revealed, Recognizing Faces and Feelings to Improve Communication and Emotional Life.* New York: Holt Paperbacks.

Fascinating book on the practical management of emotion in everyday life. Everything you always wanted to know about Duchenne smile but were afraid to ask.

Hochschild, A. R. (1983). *The Managed Heart: Commercializa tion of Human Feeling.* Berkeley: University of Cali fornia Press.

Already a classic! Using the experiences of flight attendants, the author describes the stresses and effects of on-the-job "emotional labor".

Lateiner, D. (1998). *Sardonic Smile: Nonverbal Behavior in Homeric Epic.* Ann Arbor: University of Michigan Press.

Noting differences from modern gestures and attending to variation that results from gender, age, and status, the author examines every major variety of Homeric nonverbal behavior, especially the famous sardonic smile.

Patterson, M.L. (2011). *More than Words. The Power of Non Verbal Comunication.* Barcelona: Editorial Aresta.

More than Words is an engaging, research-based discussion of the how and why of nonverbal communication, written by an internationally-known scholar. Patterson's approach, developed over forty years of research and writing, is a functional one, emphasizing the utility of nonverbal communication in social settings. More than Words provides new insight into this pervasive system of communication, not only for the novice, but also for students and scholars in the field.

Russell, J. A. & Fernández-Dols, J. M. (1997). *The Psychology of Facial Expression.* Cambridge: Cambridge University Press.

My favorite book on facial expression - fascinating and thought provoking. Lots about smiling in different social contexts!

Trumble, A. (2004). *A Brief History of the Smile.* New York: Basic Books.

A popular analysis written by Australian historian of art. The book is written in an engaging and witty style and the topics range from the holy smile of the Buddha to the Cheshire's Cat grin.

Wierzbicka, A. (1999). *Emotions across Languages and Cultures: Diversity and Universals.* Cambridge: Cambridge Univer sity Press.

A must read. In this truly ground-breaking book, an eminent Polish linguist, Anna Wierzbicka brings psychological, anthropological and linguistic insights to bear on our understanding of the way emotions are expressed and experienced in different cultures and languages.

Made in the USA
Lexington, KY
10 September 2012